Looking Back, Moving On

Applying Biblical Principles of Freedom to Your Life

Boyd Luter

NAVPRESS

BRINGING TRUTH TO LIFE
NavPress Publishing Group
P.O. Box 35001, Colorado Springs, Colorado 80935

The Navigators is an international Christian organization.
Jesus Christ gave His followers the Great Commission
to go and make disciples (Matthew 28:19). The aim of
The Navigators is to help fulfill that commission by
multiplying laborers for Christ in every nation.

NavPress is the publishing ministry of The Navigators.
NavPress publications are tools to help Christians grow.
Although publications alone cannot make disciples
or change lives, they can help believers learn biblical
discipleship, and apply what they learn to their lives and
ministries.

Library of Congress Catalog Card Number:
    92-42570
ISBN 08910-97201

Cover illustration: Matt Ambre

Some of the anecdotal illustrations in this book are
true to life and are included with the permission of the
persons involved. All other illustrations are composites
of real situations, and any resemblance to people living
or dead is coincidental.

Unless otherwise identified, all Scripture in this publica-
tion is from the *New American Standard Bible* (NASB),
© The Lockman Foundation 1960, 1962, 1963, 1968,
1971, 1972, 1973, 1975, 1977.

Luter, Boyd.
    Looking back, moving on / by Boyd Luter.
        p.   cm.
    Includes bibliographical references.
    ISBN 0-89109-720-1 : $10.00
        1. Mental health—Religious aspects—Christianity.
    2. Mental health—Biblical teaching. 3. Spiritual
    life—Christianity. 4. Luter, Boyd.   I. Title.
    BT732.4.L88   1993
    248.8′6—dc20   92-42570
                                                        CIP

Printed in the United States of America

FOR A FREE CATALOG OF
NAVPRESS BOOKS & BIBLE STUDIES,
CALL 1-800-366-7788 (USA)
or 1-416-499-4615 (CANADA)

CONTENTS

To each wounded spiritual warrior
whose personal recovery can serve as a prelude
to a merciful ministry "safe haven" for hurting believers
(and unbelievers) in the gathering storm of the 1990s

FOREWORD

When we give in to the tendency to quickly make biblical personalities into saints, we usually end up removing them from the human
race. Endowing them with halos, and a special "spiritual" glow, we
interpret their lives from the perspective of looking backward in time.
Faith seems easy with the benefit of hindsight. But that kind of easy
faith doesn't provide the important insights and strengths we need to
handle our own personal struggles with day-by-day living. When we
take away the halos and come to Scripture with fresh eyes, we can see
the genuine struggles in the lives of each of these people, and we can
learn important truths and insights that help encourage and strengthen
us in our own personal struggles with the realities of life.

In *Looking Back, Moving On*, Dr. Boyd Luter has given us a fresh
look at two of the most powerful characters we encounter in the Bible:
Daniel and Paul. If anyone had it all together, it had to be these two giants
of the faith. They faced life triumphantly, making the right choices and
taking bold positions even in the face of death. But let's not overlook the
struggles they experienced. After all, if we can see *their* humanity, we
can better accept our own humanness as a starting point in our movement
toward health, wholeness, and freedom.

I've had the pleasure of working with Boyd, and I know that the
biblical principles he describes in this book are not just some abstrac-
tion drawn from the lives of Daniel and Paul. They are also drawn from

his own life and from the lives of those he has worked with over the years as a pastor and a theologian. Finding a seminary professor who will let down his guard and open up about his own struggle with matters of faith is all too often a rare event. But there's nothing more life changing than good theology that is rooted in personal experience. And that's what you will encounter as you study and read this book.

I pray that this book will inspire the beginning, or the deeper continuation, of your own personal journey that usually begins in the pain of the past, then enters into the dynamic struggle of genuine faith in the crucible of daily life, and gradually moves on into an exciting tomorrow that is grounded in a solid faith that gives hope and freedom!

—DAVID STOOP, PH.D.
Minirth-Meier Clinic West
Newport Beach, California

PREFACE

Back in the 1980s, I wrote a commentary on Philippians for the *Evangelical Commentary on the Bible*. Since that time the phrase "forgetting what lies behind" (Philippians 3:13) has stuck to me like Super Glue.

Ironically, however, at the very time that I could not *forget* that haunting idea, I also couldn't *remember* more than a double handful of events from my own childhood.

For several years I avoided or simply laughed off any connection between the two. I now realize that I was engaged in a tenacious form of what counselors call "denial." My denial was so deep it truly amazes me that I *ever* came to the point of remembering the painful early life events I had buried so effectively, for so long, within me. But I did learn to remember in order to "forget" in a healthy way.

The circumstances in which I finally faced my denial and set out to retrieve and deal with my blocked memories are described in chapter 1 and referenced throughout the book. Although I am now well down the road of recovery, I still have trouble fathoming that I could have been so totally out of touch with the unresolved trauma and conflicts latent in my heart for all those years. After all, I am a Christian leader and seminary professor. I should know better, right?

Yet my friend and former colleague Neil Anderson has concluded that someone with my emotional profile is far from unique in ministry. He drew that conclusion from an extensive number of surveys that he took at Talbot Seminary in connection with practical theology classes. If Anderson is correct, there may well be a virtual army of those currently serving as pastoral and educational leaders in significant evangelical ministries who desperately need some type of recovery in their own lives.

My own less extensive and more informal interaction with ministerial students, colleagues in church ministry, and fellow instructors largely verifies Anderson's findings. I have written this book to address the needs of the average Christian, but my fellow-servants in vocational ministry have never been far from my mind and heart. The subject matter in the two appendices provides ample evidence of the crucial need in this area.

For those "walking wounded" in the ranks of formal and professional ministry, I emphasize my personal identification and concern by dedicating this volume to each of you. May your recovery process enhance your walk with the Lord, your family, and your ministry. May it truly transform your exhausting pastoral calling into a healthy heavenward pilgrimage! That is my prayer and heartfelt desire for all whose weariness in well-doing is as much, or more, related to confusing internal issues as to the normal wear-and-tear of ministry.

—BOYD LUTER

ACKNOWLEDGMENTS

A book like this could not be completed without considerable sacrifice and labor beyond the writer's role, not to mention invaluable stimulation and refreshing encouragement. The following are all key members of my Oscar-quality "supporting cast." I owe a huge debt of loving gratitude to each one of you that I can only prayerfully hope to repay gradually and consistently over the course of my remaining lifetime.

To Cathy, who helped a wary husband understand the need for recovery and who hung in there through the "ebb and flow" of this project.

To Joanna, Natalie, and Tim, who let Daddy stick with his writing sometimes when they didn't want to, and loved me anyway.

To my mother, Ann; my sisters, Becky and Beth Ann; and my brother, Bill—who came to understand that bringing the pain that "lies behind" in your life into healthy resolution can also benefit others.

To Joan Anderson and Heather Edwards, whose splendid secretarial skills and sunny dispositions freed me to produce the manuscript with much less stress.

To the administration of Talbot School of Theology, Biola University, who graciously allowed me to offer an elective course dealing with this subject matter in June 1992; as well as the Talbot faculty and staff, an incredibly gifted and productive team that beautifully provides "iron sharpens iron" intellectual stimulation, genuine caring hearts, and generous portions of fun and laughter.

To some friends and colleagues who went beyond the call of duty: Dr. Dennis Dirks, dean of Talbot, who cared more about me as a person than as a professor; Drs. Alan Gomes and Richard Rigsby, treasured friends *and* brothers (Proverbs 18:24); Professor Ron Glass, my former teaching assistant/team teacher, who covered my classes when I was incapacitated; and Dr. Keith Edwards, dean of Rosemead School of Psychology, whose initial wise and godly counsel helped direct me down the road to recovery.

To Grady Yarbrough, Jr., Th.M., of the Springs Counseling Center near San Antonio, Texas, my fellow alumnus, whose balanced approach to in-depth counseling accomplished more in less time than I ever thought possible, propelling me a quantum leap forward in my recovery process.

To my "maiden voyage" hearers at Trabuco Canyon Community Church and Talbot School of Theology, who wrestled with my biblical exposition of recovery on the proving ground of daily life.

To Pastor Jay Marshall and his wife, Suzanne, long-time friends and sometime counselors, whose balanced modeling of a recovery emphasis in a local church setting showed me it could be done . . . without sacrificing biblical ideals.

To Dr. David Stoop, who got me started writing about biblical recovery by including me on the editorial team of the *Life Recovery Bible*.

To Rick Christian, who, besides looking out for my best interests as a top-notch literary agent, doubles as a Barnabas-like encourager and friend.

To Steve Webb, Bruce Nygren, and the rest of the talented team at NavPress, who richly deserve their "rising star" reputation in evangelical publishing.

Above all, may the glory go to the gracious Lord of recovery, who has, in the very best sense of the word, "underwritten" this entire process!

1

WHO NEEDS RECOVERY?

Surely hitting bottom can't take me any lower than this! reasoned my feverish brain on a dark day in late September 1990. Impersonating a limp dishrag in a hospital bed for three days was not my idea of fun. But the 103-degree temperature accompanying my case of viral pneumonia would not recede. I was not only utterly miserable physically but near despair because I couldn't accomplish anything related to my work.

Over the years, the importance I placed on doing my job had subtly grown to be almost interchangeable with my sense of self-esteem. So when this serious (and, as it turned out, fairly extended) illness crippled my ability to fulfill my work responsibilities, it depressed me as well. My lagging self-image felt as rotten as my aching body.

As if things weren't bad enough, one hospital doctor insisted on conducting a "chat" about my overall health shortly after I finally began to improve. I assured him that, with rare exceptions, I never got sick beyond an occasional cold or short-term flu bug. Even more rare was when I missed work because of illness. Surely that would convince this physician that what had happened to me was merely a fluke!

FACE THE MUSIC . . . OR ELSE!

But the doctor would not agree with my self-diagnosis. In spite of my healthy track record, he warned of possibly serious future physical problems unless I made some important changes in my lifestyle. He also hinted that I might have to face and resolve some internal emotional issues.

My initial gut-level reaction to the doctor's gentle suggestion was, "Who, me? A seminary professor and former pastor? Why, I've done several thousand hours of pastoral counseling, helping others with their problems. I'm supposed to be the one with the answers, not the problems."

For all my natural resistance, though, deep down I heard the ring of truth in this man's words. In fact, several months before my illness had leveled me, I had already begun to scratch beneath the surface of some internal issues in my life.

My wife, Cathy, had introduced me to a seminar on codependency in Long Beach, California, put on by the Minirth-Meier Clinic West staff. Although some of the concepts sounded strange—even scary—to me, most of it made perfectly good sense even to the intellectualizing stoic I was at that time.

But up until my illness, not much change had taken place within me. The new ideas did prompt me to admit that I needed to understand, on a deeper emotional level, the impact of my painful childhood relationship with my dad.

My dad had died unexpectedly just before Christmas 1988, only two months after we had finally managed to "bury the hatchet" between us. I knew I hadn't worked through that loss completely—it had taken me over six months just to get past the initial numbness and be able to cry. But now these new ideas were raising the question of whether the long-ago dynamics of our troubled father-son relationship could profoundly affect my emotional and physical health as a forty-year-old man. My collapse in the hospital helped bring these issues to a head.

HEADING BACK TO HOME BASE

For nearly a month after being discharged from the hospital I was required to rest at home and recuperate. Going against my long-standing pattern of trying to be a pastoral "Superman" who blazed undeterred through whatever painful events were going on in my life or around me, I finally—and firmly—decided to begin exhuming childhood memories from their virtual burial ground in the depths of my heart. I especially needed to understand my relationship with my father, Asa Boyd Luter, Sr.

The hardest part of this process was admitting that I couldn't do it alone. A substantial part of my life was interned within me, and I didn't really have a clue to unlocking that internal vault in search of answers.

Through the gracious help of colleagues, I was able to receive assistance from a few key individuals who encouraged me to unearth my early experiences and helped draw out a route map for the recovery journey ahead. I entered a process that was to take me through successive levels of insight in succeeding months, culminating in a watershed counseling encounter in January 1991 that reoriented my life in new directions.

The process of thawing out memories I had consigned to the deep freeze was almost as painful as it was insightful and healing. It seemed as if I cried more in those last two months of 1990 than I had cried from age fifteen to forty. It's amazing how swiftly a cleansing flood is unleashed once you break the dam. But my athletic background had instilled in me the principle of no pain, no gain. And Paul's example in Philippians 3:13 gave me courage to press on to the point of greater understanding of, and release from, the past.

I gained a very clear sense of God's guidance in this process when a few "chance" contacts resulted in my appointment in late December 1991 as an associate editor for a project devoted to the application of biblical truth to the process of recovery, both in a general framework as well as in specific issues.[1] So at the same time that I was digging down into my past to identify the issues that had been impacting me, I was digging down into the Scriptures with a team of others to identify how the Bible spoke to those issues.

SEARCHING THE SCRIPTURES

My research into biblical recovery material led to an experimental preaching series. The first passages I chose were in Daniel 9 and Philippians 3.

After much prayer and consideration, I had chosen Daniel and Paul in order to counteract the prevailing stereotype that recovery was relevant only to those with alcoholic, drug abuse, or child abuse backgrounds. I wanted to demonstrate that even some of the most spiritually mature characters in the Bible had to go through what we have come to call "recovery."

For most of us, Daniel and the Apostle Paul are probably leading candidates for a "Top Ten" list of godly biblical figures. Who would we put on a list of biblical candidates for recovery? Samson, sure; Mary Magdalene, yes; maybe even Peter after his "denial" of knowing Jesus Christ. But Daniel and Paul? Not!

But when I looked at the pain in the early experiences of my life, I saw in a new way what must have been the devastating internal effects of pain or dysfunction that is observable in the lives of the godly Jewish statesman, Daniel, and the godly Jewish Christian churchman, Paul. If I needed recovery, then it was at least possible that Daniel and Paul wrestled with similar needs. And if that were true, then how many more committed, perhaps even very mature, saints of the Lord were in need of recovery as well?

These questions lead straight to the heart of this book. My aim is to establish the biblical legitimacy of the recovery process. But even more, it is to "carry to term" those biblical understandings by offering suggestions for practical applications to believers journeying through the recovery process. In Daniel's case as well as Paul's, we can mine important biblical principles while observing how they are applied to specific issues and struggles.

These biblical principles hit home to me in the process of my own struggle to understand my internal issues and learn how to deal with them. Although I gained important insights in many areas and in regard to almost all my primary relationships, certainly the most immediately "transformational" had to do with: (1) understanding my relationship to my dad and how profoundly it has impacted my current life; and (2) applying a processing, then releasing (what I've come to call "nuggets and slag") strategy to cut loose from the negative part of (thus, balancing) that impact.

Three months earlier, when I was hospitalized with viral pneumonia, I feared it was the beginning of the end in my life. But, as it turned out, the "bottom" I had hit was the starting point of the uphill climb to recovery. That dark and confusing time was the end of the beginning. It was a first step of transition to a far better understanding of my past family dynamics, of who I am as a unique member of the

Body of Christ, and of how I can have a healthy relationship with my *heavenly* Father and be the kind of *earthly* father my kids need and deserve.

But before we move into specific issues in the recovery process, let's get a general perspective on the recovery process in Christian context.

CHRISTIAN COUNSELING APPROACHES TO THE RECOVERY PROCESS

There are many Christian approaches to the recovery process currently circulating. At the risk of over-simplifying, I will describe most "Christian counselors" as falling into one of three broad categories.

1. *Scriptural counselors* use a sort of "personalized sermonizing" approach. Those in this camp generally deny the need to surface the deep pain because, in their view, applying relevant biblical passages at the surface level will accomplish whatever is needed.

2. At the other end of the spectrum is what I have heard called *secular therapists in sheep's clothing*. This group is composed of Christians who have been trained on the cutting-edge of counseling theory and therapy but tend to "trust" their psychological background almost exclusively in the counseling setting. This approach is often characterized by long-term counseling relationships that emphasize deep "self-awareness" over healing.

3. There are also various kinds of middle-ground *integration approaches* to Christian counseling. Some lean more to the biblical side of the aisle, others to the psychological side. Both sides of the aisle can field substantive critiques of the other as well as imposing lists of their own merits. Whatever the differences in approach, however, everyone in this category attempts to balance a foundational commitment to God and His written Word with the best legitimate insights of psychological theory and therapy. Depending on the counselor and the counselee's situation, therapy may be brief and to the point or much deeper and longer.

I was fortunate to work with a balanced Christian counselor who blended his own ability to identify with the counselee's personal pain and the need to get through it with reliance on the Lord and His Word, understanding of the strengths and shortcomings of modern therapy, and a methodology that gets to the heart of the matter as quickly and thoroughly as the situation warrants while moving ahead in an efficient out-patient framework of time blocks rather than hourly sessions meted out one tidbit at a time.

EVANGELICAL RESPONSES TO THE RECOVERY PROCESS

As the tidal wave of the recovery movement has risen dramatically in the last five years, there have been three basic responses to it in evangelical circles. Two of these are opposite extremes: "buying it hook, line, and sinker" (usually because it "works") over against "throwing the baby out with the bathwater" (usually because it is not obviously "biblical"). The third major reaction occupies measured middle-ground: keep the clean "baby" (i.e., the part of recovery that is biblically valid and applicable), but throw out the polluted (unbiblical) "bathwater."

With the bedrock principle of biblical discernment in mind, the first position is guilty of pragmatic uncritical acceptance. That view is not only naive, but it also presumes that if an idea works in practice it must be right, which is backwards reasoning. If a position is truly biblical, it *will* work "where the rubber meets the road." But plenty of things "work" in the short-term (e.g., speeding on the highway, little white lies, or petty theft) that aren't biblical.

On the other hand, the "throw out first, think later" approach is not much better from a discernment standpoint. Where would the Church of Jesus Christ be if doctrines such as the Trinity and the hypostatic union of Christ's Person—neither of which was *immediately* obvious from the Scriptures to the Church Fathers—had not been hammered out over time through close study and discussion? When the working assumption is that, because an idea is *new*, it is ruled out by definition, the Christian community has set itself in concrete. Certainly believers are to guard the orthodox biblical position, but not to the total exclusion of valid fresh insights.

The third position approaches both recovery and the Scriptures from the most balanced perspective. Wheat and chaff are mingled together in the recovery movement, and the unbiblical chaff must be separated from the biblical wheat with staying-power. This task is not easy, but it is important. It forms the basis of much of what we will be doing in this book.

A DEFINITION OF "RECOVERY"

It is reasonably safe to say that, at this stage, in spite of all that has been written, there is no consensus non-technical definition of recovery. This lack, along with related misunderstandings, contributes greatly to the sometimes tense differences in evangelical reactions to recovery discussed above.

In order to make "recovery" understandable to the average Christian, it is valid to parallel it to physical healing from injury or illness. In both cases it may take more or less time and means of treatment to come to the point of substantial healing and health. That is true, of course, because physical sicknesses and injuries vary greatly in intensity and impact on the victim.

After considering this helpful analogy, it is possible to offer a useful working definition. In a nutshell, *recovery is the comeback process from an unhealthy event, relationship, or behavioral pattern that continues to impact a person's life in negative ways.*

With a clearer understanding of what's at issue, believers can make informed decisions about the legitimacy and helpfulness of the various recovery approaches. Now let's look at the benefits of biblical recovery.

COUNTING THE BLESSINGS

There are at least four major benefits that evangelical Christians can receive through understanding and carefully applying a recovery perspective.

Reading the Cultural Map

The broadest of these four profit factors has to do with understanding the cultural setting in which we live in the 1990s. Some may think that the increasingly heightened cultural and subcultural tensions across the country have emerged out of thin air. However, it is much more realistic to note how incredibly warped our society has become as a cumulative result of the epidemic of recovery-related issues such as addictions and abuse.

A recovery vantage point recognizes the emotional legacy of the earlier part of the twentieth century in undermining healthy, balanced living today. For example, how did the typical stoicism of the Great Depression era, two world wars, and the Korean conflict affect the children (who are today's middle-aged and older adults) of those eras? In the hidden depths of their hearts, many of them are card-carrying stoics to this day.

The mid-to-late twentieth century hasn't been much help, either. Neither the counter-culture movements of the Vietnam War era nor the conspicuous consumption mentality of the eighties has been very emotionally healthy for our culture. Perhaps many younger (and a few older) people have learned to express their emotions more openly. But, most of what is being expressed is pain, rage, and emptiness. It is becoming increasingly obvious that recovery needs are part of a general societal malady, not just an isolated trendy phenomenon.

Passing the Family Baton

A second major plus for American evangelicals in understanding recovery has to do with the much-discussed (sometimes hotly debated) disintegration of the family in our country in recent times. Recovery honestly faces the natural transferring of behavioral and emotional baggage from one generation to the next. "Like father, like son" happens in regard to the good, the bad, and the ugly aspects of behavior.

Certainly healthy families pass on a lot of positive traits through a kind of parent-child mentoring, and recovery can greatly help bring that about. But there are more and more dysfunctional parents now bequeathing emotional and behavioral "fool's gold" to their kids. These patterns desperately need to be corrected before future generations of children continue to be emotionally and relationally maimed.

From a biblical standpoint, this progressive unraveling of the family fabric in our society is clearly related to the reverberating effects of sin from generation to generation spoken of in the Ten Commandments. Although it has never seemed fair to me that children or grandchildren would suffer because of the behavior of their forebears, it is definitely realistic. That is the bad news, which will not go away.

But the good news is that the cycle of sin and dysfunction can be broken. It has begun to happen in my life. We will also observe this decisive, then ongoing, break from the past in the lives of Daniel and Paul.

Accomplishing the Church's Priorities

Three of the most important functions that Christ designed His Church to carry out are *evangelism, edification,* and *encouragement.* Each of these three is closely tied to a biblically based approach to recovery.

As the 1990s progress, recovery will be one of the relatively few remaining open avenues for sharing the gospel of Jesus Christ in an increasingly biblically illiterate and secular culture. Christ is the "Lord of recovery" and the only power source for healing with an eternal dimension. Colossians 4:5-6 presents what is often called friendship evangelism as "scratching where they itch," or speaking to felt needs. In the years ahead, that will increasingly mean dealing with complex, longstanding recovery issues.

Edification, or Christian growth, has to do with moving from spiritual Point A (where the Lord finds us) to Point B (substantial behavioral likeness to Jesus Christ). That is precisely what a biblical approach to recovery is seeking to accomplish, and it is classically seen in the flow of Paul's thoughts in Philippians 3:7-16 (note especially the recurring use of the present tense throughout, implying an ongoing process).

Biblical encouragement must honor the commands to "weep with those who weep" (Romans 12:15) and "bear one another's burdens" (Galatians 6:2). Those scriptural responsibilities provide strong indication that the Church of Jesus Christ is to be a "haven of recovery" for those who have been shipwrecked by the storms of life (see appendix A, page 169).

Facing Personal Reality

In a very real sense, all Christians are in recovery. If that sounds odd or even heretical, remember that humanity has not been "normal"—in the sense of how God designed us to function—since the fall of humankind into sin, as recorded in Genesis 3. Ever since that point, the hereditary case of "Adam's and Eve's sin-drome" that infects each person has made us "dysfunctional" to a significant extent.

Therefore, relatively emotionally healthy believers should never view those with severe recovery-related problems as "emotional lepers." The difference between the two emotional states is merely a matter of degree, not a difference in kind.

There is a growing, and largely useful, wholistic orientation in many evangelical circles today. Among other emphases, it seeks to take into account all dimensions of human personality in balance. In that light, it is nothing less than a personal tragedy and a massively imbalanced orientation to continue denying the need to face recovery issues, which so painfully affect the emotional, spiritual, and relational planes of our existence as believers.

In part 1, we will examine the turning point of recovery by examining the life of Daniel. In part 2, we will unearth insights from the life of Paul as we examine the ongoing process of recovery.

A PRAYER
FOR
RECOVERY

2

BETTER LATE THAN NEVER

Conventional wisdom claims that "old dogs can't learn new tricks." However, I beg to differ. *Some* old hounds *can* learn new ways.

Boscoe, our family's thirteen-year-old dog, adjusted very nicely (and amazingly quickly) to our new kitten, Oreo. Frankly, we expected our canine senior citizen to be grumpy, or even pout in a corner, for a while. To our great surprise, though, Bozzie immediately wanted to play with the newest addition to the family, even if it was a cat. Wonders never cease.

In the final months of my dad's life, I saw unexpected changes take place in him. Even for the young, it's no easy task to take stock of yourself and face your weaknesses and mistakes head-on. It has to be even more difficult when you're past seventy-five, as Dad was in 1988 when he modeled his "new tricks" before my skeptical eyes.

As I think back on that relational turning point in his life, I have unbounded admiration for the courage and honesty he displayed. After over twenty-five years of either angry clashing or painful distance in our "relationship," there didn't seem to be much of a basis for burying the hatchet. That was especially true because, for the last fifteen of those twenty-five years, I had repeatedly approached Dad to try to work things out.

It is not an overstatement to say that our "cold (sometimes hot!) war" was the most consistently upsetting aspect of my life—and the most disappointing part of my walk with the Lord (as I suspect it was with Dad). Nothing made me feel more like a rank failure as a Christian than my persistent inability to get things straightened out with that man whose name I carried like a weight around my neck.

ELEVENTH-HOUR BREAKTHROUGHS

Based on past performance, there seemed to be exactly zilch likelihood that Asa Boyd Luter, Sr., would reach out to Asa Boyd Luter, Jr., for reconciliation. Particularly after our last clash a few months earlier, I wasn't going to hold my breath, for fear of turning a deep shade of blue, while waiting for him to initiate some sort of "truce." Our family history indicated that he would choose to stand pat within his shell of stubborn self-preservation, even if that was very much a *dis*comfort zone.

Imagine my shock when Dad called to ask if he (and Mom) were welcome to come visit in a few weeks . . . so that he and I could talk about what stood between us. Amazingly, I did not faint or go into cardiac arrest. Instead, I told him that I would like nothing more than to do just that, but that I would not be party to another angry face-off that solved absolutely nothing.

He readily, and humbly, agreed over the phone, then proceeded to more than live up to his word. At that vulnerable and repentant moment of our reconciliation, Dad impressed me more and made me prouder to be his son than in all the preceding thirty-nine years of my lifetime combined.

I've become increasingly convinced that the forgiveness that finally flowed freely between us as adults turned out to be my first, and very crucial, step toward recovery. After the healing of our present-tense relationship, and especially after Dad's stunning death only two months later, I could no longer focus on current "rotten fruit." It became more and more apparent that my own "roots" were clogging the emotional pipes.

Few people would suspect that Daniel, the sixth-century BC Jewish statesman and prophet, could have been on the same emotional wrestling team as my father and me. But after coming to understand what he worked through, I would nominate Daniel for Most Valuable (and Versatile) Player. In a very real sense, Daniel simultaneously occupied both roles Dad and I played as he wrestled with what we call recovery issues. He had to face the painful present reality as an outgrowth of the cumulative mistakes and societal dysfunction of the dark, distant past. The most amazing part of all this is that Daniel learned these "new tricks" well past his eightieth birthday.

To bemoan the fact that some aging person did not face his deep problems at an earlier point in life is to look at the glass as half empty. As we will see in Daniel's experience, it is much more biblical to see the glass as half full. *In facing past traumas and their present effects, it's always "better late than never" because it opens the door to future progress.*

AN IMPORTANT CLUE TO DANIEL'S RECOVERY

Great detectives are always looking for clues. For many years, I deserved an "F" in my biblical detective work related to the book of Daniel. I completely failed to notice one of the most obvious possible clues regarding a crucial over-arching emphasis of the book: *when* the recorded events occurred in the known chronology of Daniel's lifetime.

A common strategy of biblical writers for handling an open-ended subject in a compact and purposeful way is to select a limited number of related incidents that illustrate the particular themes they want to emphasize. I have used this strategy in this book by selecting a few related incidents from my life to show how my understanding and application of biblical recovery principles have grown over time.

In the case of Daniel's life, chapters 1–3 of the book of Daniel deal with his younger years (probably up to his early twenties). Daniel 4 presents a lone snapshot of the central character during middle age (probably around age fifty). Daniel 5–12 shows our hero as a senior citizen (between his mid-sixties and mid-eighties), and the bulk of that section (Daniel 5–6, 9–12) focuses on the last three recorded years of Daniel's life (539–536 BC).

The author of Daniel[1] has clued his readers into one of his major intentions by the periods in Daniel's life that he emphasizes. As table 2.1 (page 28) shows, the book "spotlights" Daniel's formative years (chapters 1–3) and advanced years (chapters 5–12). These combined proportions—over 90 percent of the book—strongly imply that the keys to Daniel's greatness as a man of God will be found in linking these sections, and particularly in understanding events that happened near the end of his long and illustrious life.

Table 2.1		
Daniel's Recovery: Trauma at Life's Bookends		
609 BC—King Josiah dies, creating instability in Judah	Over	539 BC—Daniel is endangered through, and in the wake of, "handwriting on the wall" incident
605 BC—Nebuchadnezzar invades Judah, capturing Daniel and friends	Sixty	539 BC—Medes/Persians invade Babylon, installing a new government
605–602 BC—Daniel and the others are renamed and aggressively reeducated in Babylon's wisdom and ways	Years	ca. 538 BC—Daniel almost dies in the lion's den because of Darius
ca. 603 or 602 BC—Daniel and friends almost die because of Nebuchadnezzar's dream	Between	ca. 538 BC—Daniel prays for Israel's recovery based on Jeremiah 25, 29 and Leviticus 26
(From about ages 11-18)		(About ages 81-82)

Significantly, Daniel in his older years provides the setting not only for roughly half the book (Daniel 5–6, 9–12), but also for the climactic action in both the predominantly history (chapters 1–6) and prophecy (chapters 7–12) "halves" of Daniel. The same general effect emerges when the book of Daniel is divided into its Hebrew (chapters 1, 8–12) and Aramaic (chapters 2–7) language segments. If anything, the comparison between the dramatic pain in Daniel's early years (chapter 1) and what he worked through in his twilight years (chapters 9–12) is even more accentuated by the striking shift away from, then back to, the native Hebrew of the Jewish exiles in Babylon.

THE PAIN BURIED UNDER JERUSALEM'S RUBBLE

We will be looking in depth at Daniel's "golden years." However, because we are searching for the root cause of a later problem, we will begin at the beginning. This will enable us to track the underground stream of whatever is involved throughout the process until it surfaces.

In the case of Daniel, the "beginning" of what can be known does not start with Daniel 1:1. Closely related Scripture offers additional helpful insights before that point in time.

If Daniel was taken to Babylon by Nebuchadnezzar's forces in 605 BC as a young teenager, as is almost certain, he would have been born during the reign of King Josiah, who ruled Judah from 640–609 BC.[2] That period proved to be the last hurrah for godly leadership in the nation before the Babylonian Captivity (see 2 Kings 22–23). After Josiah's untimely death, political and spiritual conditions slid downhill faster than an Olympic skier.[3]

It is quite likely that Daniel had a happy early childhood in which he was positively exposed to heartfelt Jewish worship of the Lord. Though that immediate influence would not last long, the foundational training did stand Daniel in good stead in his later years as a man of prayer.

When Daniel was deported to Babylon, it was to be a very different sort of "exchange student": to exchange his godly Jewish background and far-above-average mental ability for a totally new identity as a Babylonian wise-man-in-training at the ancient equivalent of Harvard. He would never go back to his native land, and even if he could have, all that he would have found there during the vast bulk of his time in Babylon would have been pile after pile of rubble.

Even though Daniel was not an eyewitness to the destruction and deaths in his homeland, it undoubtedly hurt him greatly. Since no direct mention of Daniel's family is found anywhere after Daniel 1:3, it is quite plausible that his other family members were still in Judah when Nebuchadnezzar's army leveled the Southern Kingdom. That would have made the pain and lingering shock many times worse. Despite his elevated standing in Nebuchadnezzar's royal court, Daniel was little more than a glorified prisoner-of-war, under great emotional trauma from events completely beyond his control.

THE CONFUSION FROM BABYLONIAN BRAINWASHING

When American prisoners of war returned from North Korea and North Vietnam, many told horrendous stories of the brainwashing techniques that had been employed to break down their resistance. Cults often use quite similar, although generally less violent, approaches to turn their marginal converts into "true believers."

Long before modern brainwashing, Nebuchadnezzar developed a hauntingly similar, and incredibly effective, approach. As described in Daniel 1, the king subtly lowered the natural resistance of the foreign students in his training program by pampering them with Babylonian royal cuisine. At first glance, it may appear that Daniel's major at Babylon U. was the literature and language of the Chaldeans. But those fields of study were actually secondary to an attempted overarching reorientation of personality.

This purpose is clarified in Daniel 1:7. The Babylonian name "assigned" to Daniel was not merely a translation of his original Hebrew name Daniel—as, say, "Paul" is the Greek equivalent of the Hebrew "Saul." Because the name Belteshazzar is a compound, including the name of the Babylonian god Bel, it was obviously an attempt virtually to wipe out Daniel's past life. He was required to carry around with him an implied recommendation of the Babylonian religious system in the name by which he would always be known in this strange new land.

Of course, Daniel never did forget his Jewish roots. It required tremendous resolve and courage on his part to maintain that identity, however. He had to take the huge calculated risk of refusing to eat the diet prescribed by the king and becoming a vegetarian out of biblical conviction and emotional self-defense.

Daniel made that decision largely because the Jewish law ruled out much of the food as "unclean." Yet, in so doing, he was also marking out clear boundaries and limits in his relationships and behavior. He was, in effect, drawing a line in the sand that said, "I will bend no further than this as a personality. This is who I am, and I will trust God to see me through."

The Lord did, of course, protect Daniel and his three young Jewish friends during their ten-day dietary probation period. They actually gained weight on vegetables and water, meaning the Lord probably miraculously shifted their metabolisms down to a much lower usage of energy. To the overseers of Daniel's training, it was an indication that Daniel and the other Jewish prodigies could not only survive but even thrive apart from the prescribed food of the king's table.

All in all, the high-powered Babylonian brainwashing program had considerably less surface impact on these godly teenagers than would have been expected. They stood their ground admirably in their beliefs and behavioral standards.

Still, it must not be forgotten that the Royal Indoctrination Program went on for three long years. No matter how strong a person is, it is impossible to be totally unaffected by prolonged exposure to an aggressive hostile environment. That is especially true for young people in their formative years, in this case the mid-to-late teens.

So, although Daniel and his young friends were not obviously undermined by their Babylonian reeducation, it is not realistic to think they were unscathed either. Most avenues they were exposed to probably rolled off like water from a duck's back. Yet as highly intelligent, but still sensitive and impressionable, teenagers they undoubtedly internalized at least a few factors that caused problems which would need to be dealt with in later years.

THE EMOTIONAL PERILS OF HIGH-ACHIEVERS

After Daniel's initial trial by food, it was out of the emotional frying pan and into the fire. If he had been watched closely in regard to what he ate, he was virtually under a microscope for his performance in formal studies.

External pressure to achieve academically is apparently not a completely modern phenomenon. Daniel and his friends were almost certainly engaged in a fierce ongoing competition with the rest of the best and the brightest to finish at the head of their class. That included what would have been a nerve-wracking oral final examination before King Nebuchadnezzar himself.

The Jewish students rose to the occasion, graduating with highest honors into a plum job as personal counselors to the king. But how much were they affected by the constant brutal competition and stress along the way?

If you are tempted to discount the stress aspect here, just consider how many Japanese children every year commit suicide because their grades don't qualify them for a certain kind of education at the next level. It happens more frequently in this country when a young person can't gain entrance into the "right" college or graduate school. Also, many who continue to rise through the academic ranks as high-achievers sooner or later "burn out" or become joyless, driven workaholics.

Besides, being a "genius" can be very lonely because there are so few people who can understand you or can talk to you "intelligently" (i.e., on your level).

After my bout with viral pneumonia in 1990, I came to the harsh realization that I had become at least a borderline workaholic. Later I came to understand that a great deal of what fueled that impulse could be traced back to the same age at which Daniel weathered the world-class academic competition in Babylon.

Admittedly, I am a long way from being Daniel's intellectual equal. However, I was a very strong student in the strongest academic class that little Raymond High School in Raymond, Mississippi, had ever produced. To this day, the number of graduate degrees and other marks of distinction earned by that small-town class of 1967 remains truly remarkable.

Add to that the athletic prowess of the class. Our team won our conference in football (a first) with a 9-0-1 record. We also dominated the conference and went to state tournament in basketball. I could cite more evidence of overall excellence, but suffice it to say that I was in a very high-achieving class. Certainly that context propelled me forward in many positive ways, but my internal uncertainties and desire to earn my dad's acceptance turned it into a highly competitive situation for me. Deeper than the competition with peers was my escalating internal struggle to be "good enough" to be acceptable, lovable, and significant.

There is, obviously, no fully objective way to X-ray young Daniel's emotional state, because it is not described for us in Daniel 1. However, if the overwhelming combination of being violently uprooted from home, taken to a strange foreign land, and entered into a high-pressure, long-term academic regimen had anywhere near the predictable impact, Daniel carried at least some painful unprocessed emotional baggage with him into later life.

MATURING AROUND A "NEAR-DEATH EXPERIENCE"

More than once I have been a scant few inches, or split seconds, from dying in a car wreck. On several occasions I recall seeing video footage and interviews on television of people who walked away from airplane crashes when many others didn't. As a pastor, I have even talked to several people who technically died en route to a hospital or on the operating table, then were brought "back to life."

All of these traumatic events have a similar effect on the people who go through them. Such "near-death experiences" are very difficult to get beyond. There may be great relief externally because you survived, but that point at which you could so easily have died is still branded on your mind's eye. The combination of sheer terror and out-of-control helplessness is almost as hard to dispose of as a birthmark or a tatoo.

Daniel and his friends faced a kind of near-death experience, as recorded in Daniel 2. Because King Nebuchadnezzar was unable to receive "instant insight" about a particular dream from his senior advisors, he vented his rage by decreeing that all the Babylonian "wise men," including the young Jews, would be immediately executed. In that day, ancient rulers were somewhat less than "enlightened" in regard to severance proceedings!

Fortunately, Daniel had distinguished himself enough in the eyes of those in ruling circles through his studies and early career to win an overnight reprieve. During what appears to have been an all-night prayer vigil with his Jewish sidekicks, God graciously revealed the dream and its meaning to Daniel. As a result of his precise and astounding interpretation to Nebuchadnezzar, Daniel was elevated to the highly responsible and influential joint role of provincial governor of Babylon and chief of the wise men.

When reading this chapter, it is easy to become preoccupied with the details of Nebuchadnezzar's dream and its significance for biblical prophecy.[4] Given the dream's astounding content, that is understandable. In the process, though, it is easy to forget that Daniel endured a terrifying countdown to execution.

In effect, Daniel was on death row that night. If he had had any appetite at all, it could have been his last meal. Since the king's bodyguards had been dispatched to execute the wise men, it is almost a sure thing that there were guards posted at the doors to cut off any escape attempts.

Daniel's miraculous interpretation of the king's dream and his subsequent career-making promotion must not allow us to gloss over in any way his close brush with death. If anything, the "relief of survival" at the last minute would have marked his life more than the "thrill of victory."

A LOUD SILENCE AT MID-LIFE

I don't remember which of my professors said it, but I'll never forget the phrase "a loud silence." It was used of a yawning absence where you would normally expect to find certain predictable elements in a progression. Sometimes what you *don't* find is as important in biblical interpretation as what you *do* find.

After what we would characterize as an adolescent phase filled with compounded emotional upheaval (including the grief and confusion of separation from loved ones), the ongoing stress of the Babylonian Merit Scholars Competition, and even a death threat from his boss, Daniel could certainly be excused if he approached his earlier adult and middle-age years somewhat tentatively. But that's where the deafening silence shows up, making it nearly impossible to get a reading of what is going on with Daniel's feelings during that extended period. Except for a lone scene in which Daniel loyally, but courageously, interprets a second dream for Nebuchadnezzar (Daniel 4), the reader is given the silent treatment over a period of roughly forty-five years.[5]

The best educated guess that can be made about these loudly silent years is that Daniel continued throughout in personal service to the various kings of Babylon, although likely in a lower profile and with less responsibility, through Nebuchadnezzar's death (until semi-retirement during Belshazzar's later reign; see 5:11,16).

Strikingly, though, unlike the record of Daniel's earlier years, there is no hint of emotional upheaval (except for the prophet's deep concern for King Nebuchadnezzar in Daniel 4:19). It is almost as if the writer wants his readers to conclude that it is smooth sailing right through that lengthy portion of Daniel's life. The implication that is left by this blend of eerie silence and relatively placid waters (Daniel 4) is that this part of the book, and the middle adult years of Daniel's life, are the calm before the storm.

BABYLONIAN *DEJA VU*

After the only mid-life pictures in Daniel's album that we get from chapters 4, 7, and 8, more than a decade slides silently downhill before the final stage of the collapse of the Babylonian Empire. At that point, experiences are forced on the now aged prophet that would have brought back to his memory both the events and the overwhelming emotions of that dark and distant formative part of his life.

If Daniel had any thoughts of easing into a dignified and uneventful "distinguished wise man emeritus" status, those illusions were shattered violently by the well-known events we normally call "the handwriting on the wall" (Daniel 5) and "the lion's den" (Daniel 6). Also during that same one- or two-year period,[6] and perhaps partly as a result of these traumatic events close at hand, Daniel undertook an intense season of scriptural study, prayer, and fasting (9:1-19) that resulted in both the phenomenal "Seventy Weeks" prophecy (9:24-27) and tremendous personal emotional resolution.

Since we will explore Daniel 9 in considerable detail in chapters 3–6 of this book, we will not handle it here. But it can adequately be understood only against the backdrop of the tumultuous events (and emotions) in Daniel 5 and 6, both of which strongly echo similar occurrences at least sixty years earlier.

VISITING A TOXIC BURIAL SITE

In the last few years the Environmental Protection Agency has levied some substantial fines against companies that failed to dispose of their toxic wastes adequately. In such cases, the toxic materials are usually improperly buried and eventually leak out and contaminate a broad area over a period of time.

Unresolved traumas and conflicts are toxic emotional material. They also can wreak havoc when they are improperly "buried." In my life, the clear lenses of 20/20 hindsight revealed it was just such a buried toxic load that had surfaced through the physical catalyst of viral pneumonia.

Perhaps the parallel is merely coincidental, but I'm convinced that there is a thread of similarity, however slender, between the painful transitional period that Daniel endured in his eighties and the emotional toxic waste disposal process I have meticulously worked through in the past couple of years—along with the similar experiences of many others I've talked to.

As the chart of Daniel's recovery (table 2.1, page 28) makes clear in overview, the great prophet faced essentially the same kind of situations and emotional issues in his latter years as in his teens. In each case, the painful, long-buried toxic memories undoubtedly bubbled to the surface in order to be cleaned up once and for all. Though his public demeanor remained placid, courageous, and unblemished during the frightening challenges in Daniel 5 and 6, this "surfacing" of locked away memories is openly manifest in Daniel 9, as we will see in the next four chapters.

DIVINE COACHING TECHNIQUE

All of the coaches I had, whether in Little League baseball or in high school football and basketball, would continue to run a given practice drill over and over until they observed that their players had finally gotten it right.

I think there is considerable reason to conclude that the Lord is the greatest "Coach" in all the universe. As the writer to the Hebrews tells us, He is, unquestionably, the best disciplinarian and trainer, and He cares deeply about the welfare of all His players.[7] And, of course, as Daniel 4 shows us, He is "on top," totally unbeatable, in all the really big games.

If the Lord is each believer's personal coach, then we do well to cooperate with His divine coaching strategy. That is the way to maximize our potential as a "spiritual athlete" as well as the effectiveness of God's entire team. Sooner or later, the Lord leads us back to the spiritual and emotional "drills" that we didn't quite get right at some earlier stage of development. And, trusting His firm but gracious hand upon our lives, we can get it down pat this time around.

All the great coaches preach that championships are won more by correctly executing the fundamentals of the sport than anything else. Legendary football coach Vince Lombardi felt it was beneficial to remind his Green Bay Packers, "Men, this is a football." Why should it be a shock that God would choose to have even a perennial "all-pro" like Daniel go back and rerun the basics from his earlier life?

FALL OF A CAPITAL, PART II: THE JERUSALEM "RERUN"

We pick up our story again in Daniel 5. If Nero earned a first place for inappropriate behavior by a ruler by fiddling while Rome burned, Belshazzar deserves at least a strong honorable mention for partying while

Babylon was falling into the hands of the besieging Medo-Persian army. More than likely, what was intended to be a kind of pep rally to help the remaining leaders of the reeling Babylonian Empire make a valiant stand (which turned out to be a lot like "Custer's Last Stand") deteriorated down a river of alcohol into little more than a drunken orgy.

With the courage of the grape fueling his inebriated thoughts, King Belshazzar, for some unknown reason, had the sacred Jewish temple vessels brought into the banquet hall to serve as drinking goblets. As far as the Lord was concerned, Belshazzar and Babylon had just tossed on the straw that broke the camel's back. God sent forth the famous "handwriting on the wall," which totally unnerved the king (5:6).

That is the point where the long-forgotten Daniel got back into the spotlight. Just as in Daniel 2, none of the other royal advisors could solve the divine riddle. So they dusted the cobwebs off the old master wise man and brought him in to provide the terrified monarch some answers. As it had happened long before, Daniel came through with the correct interpretation, although it certainly was not what Belshazzar wanted to hear. As a result, the king drafted Daniel to be the ruler just below him in the hierarchy of the Babylonian realm.

This may sound like a happy ending in a children's Bible story book, but the middle and last stanzas of this ballad were thick with danger. To continue the comparison with Daniel's earlier life, when he had to interpret Nebuchadnezzar's first dream, the king then was enraged, but apparently stone cold sober. Here Belshazzar's actions were unpredictable because he was both drunk and desperately terrified.

With the unquestioned power of life and death wielded by most ancient potentates, Belshazzar could have had Daniel exterminated at any point in their interaction—or thereafter. In his confused alcoholic stupor, "kill now and think later" would be one very likely reaction. A man as intelligent and experienced as Daniel knew that all too well.

There was also that other factor of the Medo-Persian forces knocking on the door of the one remaining Babylonian stronghold. Daniel had not been in Jerusalem when it was overrun in 586 BC, but as a ranking Babylonian official he undoubtedly knew much about the gory details. Now, much later in life, his distant fears and grief returned in an extremely "up close and personal" way. He could easily have been killed with the other Babylonian leaders.

As far as can be discerned from the biblical text (6:1-3), not only was Daniel supernaturally protected and prospered through the transition to Medo-Persian rule, he also worked through the leftover recovery issues of fear and grief that had been in suspended animation in his soul for sixty years. But those issues did not prove to be the last in the battery of final exams the Lord had in store for Daniel.

SILENCE OF THE (LAMB-LIKE) LIONS

As chapter 6 reveals, perhaps less than a year later Daniel found himself guest of honor at a very different banquet: a literal Lion's Club all-you-can-eat meal with vintage aged prophet as the main course. As a result of his consistent and vital prayer life, Daniel violated a temporary, but still unretractable, regulation signed by the Medo-Persian ruler Darius. The whole situation was nothing more or less than a preemptive scam pulled off by Daniel's rival bureaucrats to prevent the godly Jew from being promoted to chief administrator over the newly annexed province of Babylon.

How much these dynamics must have reminded Daniel of the intense competition of his early school days in Babylon! He would, of course, have the last laugh in this case. Yet, in the meantime, whatever residual resentments and frustrations may have lodged in Daniel's soul over the years likely took the elevator to the surface during this crisis. God's "back to the basics" coaching philosophy had done its job again!

Daniel's time in the lion's den and the positive aftermath are also excellent examples to those who, because of their own difficult experiences, doubt the reality of God's power working in biblical recovery. If the Lord can render lions as harmless as lambs, He can transform even the most ferocious candidate for recovery. If an entire context of "abusers" can receive their just due, after getting away with their atrocity in the short-term, there is realistic hope that such dysfunctional personalities today can be stopped from preying on those who are helpless and without protection.

ROUSING SLEEPING DOGS

If old dogs really can't learn new tricks, then maybe it would also make sense just to "let sleeping dogs lie." But since old dogs like Boscoe, my dad, and Daniel did indeed internalize some new ways, why should older believers (or others) in need of recovery snooze through their God-given opportunity?

A readily available strategy for denying or avoiding painful recovery-related issues is to maintain a state of spiritual and emotional drowsiness until it is too late. In that regard, it is entirely possible to sleep your (shot at a renewed) life away.

The next chapter will begin consideration of Daniel's heart-expanding "Prayer for Recovery" recorded in chapter 9. The details of that discussion will fill in many of the gaps of the overview treatment in this chapter.

Have you posted a sleeping guard-dog at the door to the locked-away memories of your painful past? Get ready for him to be roused! He could be sleeping in the way of your release from the bondage of unresolved past issues or relationships that are struggling to surface in your life—just as they were in mine.

3

BIBLICAL STUDY
AND DEEP RECOVERY

It has been only a few years since I used to think the human personality was like the typical lake I grew up around in Mississippi: shallow and almost always muddy. But now, with what I have learned through my own recovery process and more sensitized biblical study, I think the human personality is like the lakes in the Texas Hill Country where I once pastored: deep and, potentially, crystal clear.

What has made the difference in my perspective? More than anything else, it has been realizing that what I took for the "mud bottom" of my personality was really a "cover" I had placed over the deeper recesses of my soul to protect it from further pain.

It wasn't that I was deliberately trying to hide my personality. I didn't know myself well enough as a unique person to do something that cunning or sophisticated. It was just the only way I could squeeze into an emotional flak jacket for self-defense.

WHAT'S GOING ON DOWN THERE?

Just a few weeks ago, a friend from our home church, Roy Becker, invited my son Tim and me to go fishing on a local lake. I accepted the invitation, but it was mostly because of Tim's excitement. I did not have positive childhood fishing memories—meaning, among other things, that I hardly ever caught any fish.

On my rare fishing trips with Dad, it was always hot and sticky (normal Mississippi summer weather), and we could never figure out where the fish were biting. Frankly, though, I don't think hot and steamy would have fazed me if I could have had insight beneath the surface to track down those elusive fish.

It was a whole different ballgame with Roy Becker. He had a sonar fish-finding device on his boat that evened the score with those wily fish. The advantage of knowing what's going on beneath those gentle waves can make for a very successful outing. It was so nice to head back with more than a sunburn to show for hours of floating around on the surface.

This chapter is not going to be a collection of fish stories. But we are going to do a little "fishing" in the depths of the human personality in order to discern what's under the often murky surface. It makes a decisive difference to understand what's going on down there.

REARRANGING THE DECKCHAIRS

Before jumping into the relationship between biblical study and in-depth recovery, we need to understand the liabilities of basing personal application or counseling approaches on the kind of "shallow and muddy" perspective on personality that I had for so long.

If I simply water-ski across the surface of my life, I will never be comfortable in receiving (or giving) counseling that probes beneath the exterior appearance of things. But this surface exterior can be highly misleading (see the discussion of the Apostle Paul's "front" in chapter 7).

Make no mistake. It is entirely possible to be a Christian and live with this basically flat, one-dimensional concept of human personality. I did it for almost twenty years, with no more sub-surface insight than an emotional Mr. Magoo, the virtually blind cartoon character.

For resistant surface-floaters like me, it often takes a sinking ship to get our attention. But sometimes our response to danger is simply rearranging the deckchairs—which, of course, is a pointless exercise, because the main problem is so much deeper. Too often, it is only when our lives have reached an emotional drowning point that we recognize that the Lord's intended biblical application is targeted considerably beyond our role as conscientious deckchair custodian.

APPLICATION BY AUTOMATIC PILOT

A key factor in our response is whether we dig deep in our efforts to apply biblical truth or whether we allow the application process to run on automatic pilot.

By way of illustration, let's take a look at how many believers apply a key passage in Hebrews 4:12. It is quite plausible that the writer of Hebrews had passages such as Daniel 9, which point to the centrality of the Scriptures, in mind when he wrote these words:

> For the word of God is living and active and sharper than any
> two-edged sword, and piercing as far as the division of soul
> and spirit, of both joints and marrow, and able to judge the
> thoughts and intentions of the heart. (Hebrews 4:12)

In Daniel 9 the Scriptures do indeed pierce to the heart of the matter in the prophet's life. But it's important to note that it does not happen *automatically*. Let's take a brief side-trip to the context preceding this verse to get a clearer understanding.

In Hebrews 3:7–4:11 the writer is clearly doing a running explanation and application of Psalm 95:7-11. Twice he picks up on the usage of "today" in Psalm 95:7. In both cases (Hebrews 3:13-15 and 4:7) he employs "today" practically, urging his readers to act upon the warning in Psalm 95 without further delay.

Notice that the writer of Hebrews does not expect the truth in Psalm 95 simply to "do its thing" in the lives of the readers, just by hearing the passage from the Scriptures. He challenges them to "be diligent" (4:11) in their application. His approach to getting the transforming biblical truth into readers' lives is anything but passive.

Amazingly, even though Hebrews 4:12 is the very next verse, and obviously is intended as an explanation of the power behind the scriptural transformational process, the overall point of the wider context is often completely forgotten in evangelical proof-texting. Many Christians habitually employ verses such as Hebrews 4:12 to justify their approach of waving a couple of verses over a problem and expecting that to take care of things.

It seems to me that this use of proof-texting betrays a surface approach to human personality combined with an automatic-pilot angle on application. In effect, it assumes that application is as simple as getting out of the way of the Scripture so that Scripture can, virtually on its own, make whatever adjustments are necessary in a person's life. No fuss, no bother. Just expose yourself to the biblical truth and the divinely designed changes will follow as a matter of course.

Does this sound like an oversimplification? Try doing some sampling of your own in the days ahead. Look around in your Christian circles at how the transition from truth to practice is carried out in sermons, Sunday school classes, or Bible studies, and make some mental notes. How much challenge to active, hard-nosed personal application do you observe?

I'm not suggesting that certain Christian leaders or churches are "soft" on application (as they consciously understand application). But in many circles (certainly not all), the prevailing view is inadequate, more like a half-baked meal than a fully cooked one.

Auto-Pilot Counseling

It's unfortunate that this hit-and-run approach to biblical application shows up in numerous evangelical pulpits and classroom settings. But it's really tragic when it's employed in counseling hurting people. That is the emotional and spiritual equivalent of putting a Band-Aid on a cancer.

Over the years in my experience as a pastoral counselor, I've covered my share of malignancies with plastic strips. But like many practitioners, I considered myself to be trusting the piercing power of God's written Word. I simply didn't know any better.

In this mistaken approach, counselees who are confused and quite possibly crushed by the burdensome problem at hand are usually given a rapid-fire surface diagnosis, prescribed a few verses to take when feeling weak, and dismissed with a parting pat on the head. They're also left with the impression that if they dare to admit that this shallow "treatment" doesn't do the job at the point of deep need, it means they're not "trusting the Lord or the promises in His Word"!

It would seem that the ongoing thirst for "in-depth" Bible study and expository preaching in conservative Christian circles would stimulate demand for "biblical consistency" across the board. By that I mean that application would be as in-depth as interpretation, and counseling approaches would seek to set off "depth-charges." This consistency would show that auto-pilot application and counseling is actually unbiblical (or, at least, not *totally* biblical) while revealing the need for a careful, biblically oriented "deep recovery" approach.

DANIEL AND DEEP BIBLICAL RECOVERY

When we last saw our hero, Daniel, he had emerged from the lion's den to live out the rest of his life in well-deserved peace and quiet, right? Not by a long shot! If anything, Daniel's period of "fasting, sackcloth, and ashes" (Daniel 9:3), which was in close proximity to the lion's den episode,[1] was probably the most powerful emotional catharsis in his life up to that point.[2]

How did Daniel manage to get himself in the path of another emotional volcano so soon? By refusing to leave well enough alone. At this point in his spiritual and emotional growth, he could not be content with surface application—that is, just waiting for the living and active Word of God to crank up and carry the day by itself. Instead, he followed the standard procedure for success in petroleum exploration: if you're convinced that there is oil down there and you don't strike it at one level, drill deeper. Sure, it may be more costly. But the effort is more than worth it when you bring in a gusher.

Chapter 9 shows us Daniel's balanced model of in-depth biblical study, followed immediately by equally in-depth prayerful application. In his prayer to the Lord of recovery, Daniel links himself with the sinners of past generations (note the repeated use of "we") in breaking denial and confessing the patterns that brought about the Babylonian Exile.

The principle underscored in this chapter is central throughout the rest of this book. It is absolutely crucial for a recovery process to be truly biblical. As Daniel models, *deepening scriptural understanding should ignite prayers for recovery from the damaging effects of the past.*

A PRESSING NEED FOR DEEP APPLICATION

The time frame in which Daniel, as the newly appointed Medo-Persian commissioner under Darius, chose to do his Bible study in Jeremiah is intriguing. It seems to indicate a powerful conviction on Daniel's part that no aspect or depth level of scriptural application could be spared.

That is, he apparently operates with the sense that the full range of God's biblical promise will not come about unless its hearers fully hold up their applicational end of the deal.

This incident occurred very close to the time when Cyrus, the Persian king,[3] issued a proclamation allowing the Jewish people in Babylon to return to Jerusalem and rebuild the Temple.[4] Both that royal decree and the time frame of Daniel 9:1 occurred in the early months of transition to the Medo-Persian Empire, after the defeat of the Babylonians (see 5:30-31).

Certainly Daniel would have been delighted that his people were being allowed not only to return to their homeland, but also to begin reconstruction of their holiest site. He would not have been surprised, though. In the ascendancy of the Persian king, Cyrus, Daniel would have recognized the hand of God bringing about the fulfillment of the precise prophecy in Isaiah 44:28–45:4, made about a century and a half earlier. For alert readers of Isaiah in Daniel's day, there was very little room to misconstrue what was going on.

What would have caught Daniel off-guard was not the *fact* of Cyrus' action in sending the Jews back to the Promised Land, but the *timing* of the proclamation. Daniel knew Jeremiah's prophecy that the length of the Babylonian Captivity would be seventy years.[5] But even from the earliest possible point of reckoning—the deportation of Daniel and his friends to Babylon in 605 BC—it had been only sixty-six or sixty-seven years at the point in time in Daniel 9.

Since all this was happening well before the expected time, Daniel was undoubtedly concerned about whether his people were adequately prepared to go back to Judah. After all, it had been less than a year since the fall of Babylon to the Medes and Persians. The sense of equilibrium had probably not been fully restored in Babylon, and now the Jewish populace was being asked to consider another major transition.

Another, and even more troubling, question grew in Daniel's mind and heart as he continued to review Jeremiah 29 carefully. Were his Jewish brethren anywhere close to being *spiritually ready* to go back? He would have been particularly troubled about the condition in Jeremiah 29:12-13—praying "with all your heart" (29:13).

That so many Jews chose to remain in Babylon instead of returning to their homeland attests to the "half-hearted" commitment of a sizable portion of the Babylonian Jewish community.[6] And even those who returned may have done so for nationalistic, ethnic, or personal reasons that were not what the Lord intended at all.

What did the Lord expect in this situation? Daniel began to follow the "paper trail" of Scripture that started with Jeremiah's prophecies and ended in the deep and painful application of Daniel 9:3. In between, there is a step in Daniel's study process not reflected in Daniel 9:2. However, it is very much evident in Daniel's actions in 9:3 and his lengthy prayer in 9:4-19.

DANIEL'S PRAYER LIFE

Before peeking over Daniel's shoulder to understand what he learned from his in-depth biblical study beyond Jeremiah that influenced his prayer, it is worth noting that Daniel was anything but a fox-hole prayer warrior.

Of course, if all you noticed about Daniel's prayer life had to do with crisis situations (e.g., Daniel 2, 9, and 10), you might conclude that he prayed only when he was under the gun. But that would be a thoroughly wrong impression! Daniel 6:10 indicates that the godly prophet prayed like clockwork, three times each day. Since Daniel 6 took place within no more than a few months of Daniel 9, he most likely was planning to have his normal three periods of prayer the very day he was studying Jeremiah 25 and 29.

No, the great prayer in Daniel 9 is not the product of a surge of fear-based adrenaline. It is, rather, the heartfelt outpouring of a seasoned prayer veteran who put his vast experience in prayer on red alert because of the deep need that he concluded had to be faced immediately.

A similar situation occurred in connection with the tragic riots in Los Angeles in the spring of 1992. Many police officers and firefighters who had just finished their shifts were suddenly called back for a much longer and more dangerous period because of a situation that had been smoldering for years had reached a flashpoint. Although these officers were only doing their duty, the riot circumstances made it much more taxing than usual.

Daniel was also simply doing his duty. Yet he appears to have been a one-man force, taking on a tragic situation that had been deteriorating not just for years, but for centuries. Even if he was alone in his painful time of prayer, Daniel knew that what matters in prayer is not so much the person *asking* as the Person *answering*. With the Lord, any believer can constitute a prayerful majority. Daniel did not have to undertake a lonely prayer vigil because the Lord was with him throughout that entire wrenching time.

DOING WHAT NEEDS TO BE DONE

Have you ever wished you could be a fly on the wall of some great person's office, just to see how that individual really operates in private? Call it vain curiosity or "none of your business," but I would be fascinated to see how some people work, what makes them tick, and whether "what you see is what you get."

My fantasy will probably never happen in the workaday world, but in a sense it has been fulfilled through my opportunity to observe Daniel. As he studies and wrestles with the Scriptures, it is not at all difficult to track his thoughts and emotions. When he springs to action in heartfelt prayer and fasting, it is quite obvious where he is coming from. Although Daniel is anything but a spiritually and emotionally shallow person, he truly is a transparent one.

What Daniel read in Jeremiah 25 and 29 pointed him back to the Jewish law (see table 3.1, page 49), as the references to "the curse," "calamity," and "the law of Moses" in his prayer indicate. The main passages Daniel considered were undeniably Leviticus 26 and Deuteronomy 28 and 30 because of their warning that the Jewish people could be banished from the Promised Land as the ultimate curse.[7] The procedure and, at least as important, the attitude that the Lord required for Israel to be restored to the land is the concluding "crown" of both passages.

It appears that Daniel understood Leviticus 26:40-41 and Deuteronomy 30:1-6 as "filling in the blanks" for what seeking the Lord "with all your heart" meant in Jeremiah 29:13. The factors of confession, humility, and obedience before the Lord leap out of those passages in the Law as crucial primary applications.

Surprise! Those things are exactly what Daniel emphasizes in his following prayer (9:4-19). He is intent that Israel will not just return to the Promised Land (and perhaps to the same old dysfunctional spiritual patterns), but will return forgiven and restored according to God's standards. As a result, he does everything he possibly can to make sure that his prayer is simultaneously "by the book" and "from the heart."

Table 3.1
Daniel Digging Deeper: Scripture Fueling His Prayer

STEP ONE—SERIOUS STUDY (Daniel 9:2)
    Jeremiah 25:11-12
        Judah, desolate for seventy years, then it's Babylon's turn
    Jeremiah 29:10-11
        Judah goes home after seventy years
    Jeremiah 29:12-14
        God's people pray "whole-heartedly" and are restored

STEP TWO—FOLLOW-THROUGH STUDY (Unstated, but undeniable)
    Leviticus 26:14-45
        Progressively worse "curses" for disobedience
    Leviticus 26:34-39
        Promised Land keeps Sabbath(s) while people are in exile
    (2 Chronicles 36:21
        Seventy-year exile = Seventy sabbatical years)
    2 Chronicles 26:40-45
        People confess personal sin and forefathers' sin, then God will
        bring them back to the land
    Deuteronomy 28:15-68
        Curses (see Leviticus 26); restoration, prosperity, and change
        of heart (see Jeremiah 29:12-13)

STEP THREE—FOLLOW-THROUGH APPLICATION (Daniel 9:3)
    Prayer (as Jeremiah 29:12-13 and Leviticus 26:40-41 required)
    Fasting (humility, recovery—see Isaiah 58:5,8)
    Sackcloth and ashes (mourning, grief)

LONG-DELAYED GRIEF

In the introductory chapter, I revealed how long it took me to come to the point where I could grieve over my dad's death. I simply could not face the great sense of loss, even though Dad and I had never been close. At the time, my extremely narrow emotional range repressed that loss with a vengeance. Because it was tied up with so much of the other pain from my earlier life, it had to be held in check at all costs.

That long-term subconscious strategy worked for a while. But it finally became so obvious that even *I* couldn't deny it any longer: I had to come to terms with my past relationship with my dad in order to "press on" with the rest of my life.

Over the next two years I slowly and grudgingly began to face the pain in growing increments. It was very hard. I did not want to do it. I still have days when I want to retreat to the emotional "bunker" that got me through all those years. But the overall outcome has been worth it many times over. Now I can have a future without the albatross of past pain and dysfunction always hanging around my neck.

My continuing study of Daniel 9 has convinced me that the revered statesman-prophet had a somewhat similar experience with grief. Certainly his grief would have been great and he had a lot more to mourn that I did. He had lost not only his entire family but also an entire civilization and the central place of worship of the one true God. But through the "handwriting on the wall" and the "lion's den" confrontations (Daniel 6), this great man of God took the opportunity to deal with some of the stored-up pain of the past. Now, as the Jewish remnant was heading back to what was left of Judah, he had the chance to face off with the troubling role of his ancestors and their sin in the painful outworking of the Babylonian Exile.

Would Daniel open himself up to get out the deep pain? Would he be able to grieve fully both what he (and many others) had lost in Judah, as well as what he had needlessly endured in his earlier and later years in Babylon?

"Yes" on both counts! The "fasting, sackcloth and ashes" that were the context of Daniel's prayer were not for show. After his intensive Bible study, Daniel was equally serious about applying what he had found out from the Scriptures regarding the exiles' responsibility for confession, humility, and obedience. Prayer was the demonstration of obedience to God's Word, fasting was a sign of humility, and the sackcloth and ashes were meant as a genuine indication of grief (see table 3.1). As best as can be discerned from these actions and the prayer that follows, Daniel was holding nothing back in his quest for personal and national recovery.

A PASSIONATE, ORDERLY PRAYER

Long before the Apostle Paul recorded his far-reaching principle in 1 Corinthians 14:40, Daniel was also deeply concerned to handle things "properly and in an orderly manner." That is seen throughout his life, but it definitely includes his prayer for recovery (9:4-19). Table 3.2 shows that his thoughts flowed from the divine and human partners in prayer (9:4-6), to deep honest confession about the impact of Judah's multi-generational sin (9:7-13), to the request for reconciliation with God and restoration to the Promised Land, in order to rebuild Jerusalem (9:14-19).

Table 3.2
The Basic Flow of Daniel's Prayer of Confession

INTRODUCTION: PARTNERS IN RECONCILIATION (verses 4-6)
- Who our God is (verse 4)
- What we have done (verses 5-6)

FACING THE FACTS: TRUE GUILT AND RIGHTEOUSNESS CONSEQUENCES (verses 7-13)
- Openly ashamed, Daniel (representing denying generations) meets with his righteous and forgiving God (verses 7-10)
- Paying the price for breaking God's Law (verses 11-13)

REQUESTING RECOVERY FROM GOD: FORGIVENESS AND RESTORATION (verses 14-19)
- We honestly deserved the exile (verse 14)
- But You have helped Your displaced people before (verse 15)
- Exercise compassion and clear Your name by restoring Your people and Jerusalem (verses 16-19)

Don't assume, however, that just because Daniel's prayer is a model of orderliness, it has no fervor. Nothing could be further from the truth! Daniel's appeal to the Lord of recovery is as passionate as it is well-ordered. Those may seem to be mutually exclusive categories to some people. But both purpose and passion are necessary to accomplish the deep, heartfelt healing that is blessed by God.

Prayers are like streams. Some of them are like the lazy, shallow streams I played in as a child: a little depth once in a while, but primarily superficial, with little movement or vitality. Others are like the flooded streams I remember so vividly in the Texas Hill Country: plenty of power; but, with few restraints, they run out of bounds and cause real problems in the process.

When it wasn't flood time, those same streams in the Hill Country had both power and boundaries in balance. They were deep and fresh and alive, and proved very useful not only for agricultural purposes, but also for fishing and whitewater sports.

It is very possible to have such power and boundaries hand-in-hand in praying for recovery. In fact, as I stated earlier, it is necessary to get this "dynamic duo" working together to maximize the biblical recovery process. May "whitewater praying"—deep, clear, and moving—become a cherished sport of those seeking biblical recovery!

THAT WONDERFUL PERSONAL PRONOUN

As Daniel begins his amazing prayer, there is a beautiful balance in his description of God between His "great and awesome" attributes and His covenant lovingkindness. He really is "totally awesome," but He is just as loyal and personal to His people. Daniel confidently calls Him "the Lord *my* God" in reflection of that personal relationship.

Some Bible teachers assert that it is very hard to believe that God is simultaneously "way out there" (transcendent) and "up close and personal" (immanent). However, there is no tension here between these two sides of God's Being. I suspect that was because, in spite of the long-term pain locked up inside him, Daniel was genuinely a man of faith and prayer who relied on both the greatness and closeness of the Lord day after day. Likely because of his childhood training during the reign of godly King Josiah, it never occurred to Daniel to look at God any other way.

Sadly, this is not the case with most people who need recovery today. They were not raised in a time of revival by godly parents. Usually their version of a "father figure" is distant, absentee, or virtually non-existent. As a result, they struggle greatly with the concepts of closeness and intimacy, perhaps most of all with God. Likewise, the idea of covenant loyalty sounds like something from another planet to someone who has grown up in a broken home or been orphaned.

That's why it's so important to actively model our prayers for recovery after the *super*natural balance evident in Daniel's prayer instead of the *natural* way of looking at things.[8] For Christians who grew up in a dysfunctional home setting, as is true of so many believers I've met in the last two years, continuing to "do what comes naturally" in prayer could seriously stunt their emotional and spiritual growth.

BLOWING IT BIG-TIME

I'm honestly not sure which has affected my vocabulary more: having three children who bring home current slang or just living in the pop culture of Southern California. Whatever the reason, from time to time I hear myself cut loose with a "like totally, dude" or "blowing it big-time."

When I stop and think about it for a moment, though, some of those phrases do carry meaning. Of course, there are mindless sayings along the order of "like totally, dude" that are basically harmless filler. It gives you something ready to say when you don't have anything witty prepared. And it's preferable to the kind of expletives that often ought to be deleted.

On the other hand, a description like "blowing it big-time" says something substantive. It's an updated version of colorful phraseology from years gone by, such as one of my personal favorites: "messing up royally."

Whatever your generational vernacular, this particular phrase describes the basic verbal picture Daniel paints in 9:5. In piling up the related concepts of sin, iniquity, wickedness, rebellion, and turning aside from God's standards, Daniel freely acknowledges that Israel had blown it big-time. What may once have been an occasional raindrop of little white sin became, over the generations, a destructive torrential rainstorm of almost unbroken spiritual wickedness and rebellion. Finally, the ground of the sin-soaked nation was simply washed away by the intensifying Babylonian invasions.

This is not to say that the various words for sin in Daniel 9:5 do not present important shades of meaning and angles on Judah's transgression of God's Law. However, the cumulative effect is clearly what Daniel wished to emphasize. As much as anything, Judah had buried herself under the growing weight of her sin in many different shapes and forms. The only real questions had been when she would "die" and who would be the agent of burial.

Much as Daniel calls it like it is in confessing the sin of his people but includes himself among those responsible, when we are dealing with recovery issues we also must face the spiritual and emotional facts. Even if we have been a largely innocent victim, as Daniel certainly was in being taken to Babylon in the first place, we still must come to terms with the impact of sin on our life and relationships. Otherwise, there can be no freedom from those ongoing effects.

EARS OF STONE:
THE PROTECTIVE MECHANISM OF DENIAL

In recent decades, development of protective gear and apparel for use on the athletic field and in the workplace has increased. These advances improve safety around powerful machinery and in competition among bigger and stronger athletes.

There are, obviously, helpful protective factors in emotional recovery issues. However, not everything that is "protective" is good. In Daniel 9:6 the prophet freely admits that his people have been guilty of not listening to the other prophets God had sent to them. Whether leaders or common people, Judah as a whole had turned a deaf ear to the Lord's spokesmen.

Short of actual deafness, the literal failure to hear can occur for other reasons. I'm living proof of that assertion. A few years back, my wife became concerned about my hearing. My dad had lost some of his hearing as he had gotten older, and I had prolonged ringing in my ears after U.S. Army training in the early seventies at the field artillery school in Fort Sill, Oklahoma. So it seemed there might be legitimate cause for concern.

Before long, I had the opportunity to see an ear, nose, and throat specialist, who also happens to be a longstanding friend. He brought in the test results and immediately said, "There is absolutely nothing wrong with your physical hearing. If the sound is not getting through, it is because you are tuning it out at a deeper point in the process."

Unfortunately, I had to admit he was right, although it was quite embarrassing. Over my years of doing a good bit of my writing and preparation for outside speaking at home, I had learned to concentrate on my work in spite of many distractions. But I had not developed a way of "screening" what engaged my physical hearing so that the important and personal messages got through while the unimportant trivia got blocked out. Instead, I simply put in my nonphysical "earplugs" and tuned out almost everything around me.

Likewise, the populace of Judah wasn't open to what the prophets of the Lord were saying to them because it spoke so forcefully to their comfortable, sinful habits. Over time, they developed a societal case of spiritual hardening of the hearing mechanism. In a completely nonphysical, but still very real, sense, Judah had developed "ears of stone." They were protected from hearing what they did not *want* to hear, but they also could not hear what they *needed* to hear. Just as I was ashamed of my self-taught "deafness," so Daniel's people were brought to the point of great ongoing shame, as we will discuss in the next chapter.

OPENING YOURSELF TO DEEPER INSIGHTS

Does it still seem farfetched to you that someone like Daniel could be so dramatically affected by a deepened understanding and application of familiar Scripture after many years of exemplary living? If so, consider the classic example of Martin Luther, widely considered to be the father of the Protestant Reformation.

After taking vows as a Catholic priest, Luther continued his studies and soon became a professor of biblical studies at the University of Wittenburg in Germany. For several years, Professor Luther taught the Apostle Paul's grand letter to the Romans as a part of his course rotation.

Through understanding the foundational truth of justification by faith in Jesus Christ alone, primarily from Romans, Luther was converted to a new understanding. That set in motion not only the Reformation, but much of what has become the evangelical Christian movement in our day and time.

What is crucial for us to see is that Luther already knew Romans very well, from teaching it repeatedly at Wittenburg U., before it ever had its major transforming impact on his life. Something very similar happened when Daniel studied Jeremiah's well-known prophecy. And I remain convinced that I went through much the same deeper insight tied to a "depth charge" application sequence in regard to Philippians 3, a passage I also knew exceedingly well.[9]

A concluding riddle: What do an ancient part-time Jewish prophet, a German university lecturer of the later medieval period, and a modern evangelical seminary professor have in common? Answer: All needed and received the kind of fresh, deeper insight from Scripture and in-depth application that is at the heart of what I call "biblical recovery."

Admittedly, Daniel, Luther, and Luter constitute a small sampling for your consideration at this stage. But as you observe the Apostle Paul and others on the road to recovery throughout this book, it may well be that the Lord will begin to clarify issues about which you have been in denial, as I was for so long. Are you open to the kind of transforming insight and application that He may have in store for you?

GETTING BEYOND
A SHAMEFUL SITUATION

I was basically a very compliant child and adolescent. By that I mean that I rarely did things that were dangerous or clear violations of behavioral standards set by my parents and teachers. Still, there are some things from that now-recaptured part of my life that I'm ashamed of.

Since confession really is good for the soul—as this chapter will develop from Daniel 9:7-13—I will list a few of these "shameful" acts from my teenage years. Some of these dastardly deeds had witnesses (or "accomplices," whichever is most appropriate). Others were private. Some were pretty stupid and funny. Others, equally stupid, were very sad . . . and still are to this day.

THE FRIVOLITY OF YOUTH: A SELF-PORTRAIT

On several occasions my brother Bill and I created our own motorized golf "cart" by riding a motorcycle around the section of the local municipal golf course away from the clubhouse just before sundown so that we could play faster (and free). I shudder to think what would have happened if the golf pro had ever nailed us!

That motorcycle, normally used for delivering an early morning paper route, also served as transportation for a few lengthy excursions that I never got permission to take. Once I was caught dead to rights when I passed a family member on a city street twenty miles from home.

It was embarrassing to be an "Identified Non-Flying Object."

It was considerably more embarrassing, and the source of much internal shame, to be the only *unidentified* member of an ill-fated expedition that set out to roll our English teacher's yard with toilet paper after a senior party. The "brains" of the Class of '67 thought we had planned the perfect practical joke. But we had hardly arrived on the scene when a quiet-shattering shotgun blast by our teacher's husband put an end to our fun. We were scared to death as we sped away from what now seemed very much like the scene of a crime.

Of the three guys and three girls who set out on that comedy of errors, I was the only piece of the puzzle that our teacher never figured out (to my knowledge). Amazingly, nobody ratted on me, and I never did have to answer to the wrath of Mrs. Harris, although I lived in mortal fear of being found out for a long time.

FROM THE RIDICULOUS TO THE SAD

The final shame-inducing situation I'll mention from my deep, dark past is the saddest and most telling. I didn't date much in high school, mostly because I was terrified of being turned down when I asked a girl to go out. As a result, I only got beyond "first base" with one girl.

A cute girl had transferred from another school, and we developed a sort of distant "crush" that was mediated by friends. We actually dated only a couple of times before she got seriously ill and was absent from school for what seemed like forever.

That period of illness set off what I now realize was an unhealthy "shame-reaction" on my part. I blamed myself for her being sick. Why? My astounding (il)logic was that she had gotten sick only after she began to get closer to me. I was the apparent cause—her "jinx."

But I never told her what I was feeling, or that I had made a tortured decision to end our "puppy love" relationship. Even though I would often drive out and park at a point (beside an old Confederate Army graveyard, no less) where I could see her house in the distance and brood over *my* loss, I essentially gave *her* the silent treatment.

What a jerk I was! And what a fool in my own reasoning: I didn't want her to hurt physically from illness, so I hurt her and myself emotionally! Then I played the stoic on the outside because I was too afraid and ashamed to face her and admit my internal turmoil. As a result, there was never any resolution to that painfully unnecessary stanza in my life.

As I now look back on that time over twenty-five years in the past, I wonder how I could possibly have thought and felt what I did. But, there is no denying that I *did* think and feel those things very deeply at that juncture. Also, there is nothing to be gained from denying that they remained with me long-term as unprocessed internalized shame.

THE PARALYZING POWER OF SHAME

Just a couple of years ago, it would have been nearly impossible for me to write—or even speak guardedly—about this sort of thing. The uneasiness, embarrassment, and shame would have been overwhelming, if not paralyzing. These memories would also have resonated agonizingly with the self-portrait of a highly flawed and unacceptable person that I had painted of myself during those formative years.

During the ensuing time, though, I have discovered two important things that have enabled me to unearth the shame I had buried alive inside my soul: (1) how unhealthy—personally, interpersonally, and as my bout with viral pneumonia so graphically demonstrated, physically—such ongoing denial of shame really is; and (2) how widespread the problem of unprocessed shame is.[1]

A close reading of Daniel 9:7-13 indicates that Daniel was wrestling with the issue of shame in a remarkably similar way to many believers in need of recovery. As a result, the overarching principle taught in this passage has direct application to many such people: *It's a real "shame" that ongoing denial keeps us from confessing and receiving God's compassionate forgiveness.*

THE CRUCIAL VALUE OF CONFESSION

In Daniel 9:4 the prophet says that he "prayed to the LORD my God and confessed. . . ." This initial mention of confession sets the tone for most of this marvelous extended prayer.[2] As table 3.2 (page 51) shows, the "body" of Daniel's prayer is confession, picking up on the emphasis begun in the prayer's introductory portion.

The lack of direct mention of confession in the prayer itself should not be taken as decisive in any way. Not only does 9:4 lead in to Daniel's prayer by closely linking "prayed" and "confessed," but 9:20 effectively sandwiches the actual prayer with a confession emphasis.[3] Although "supplication," meaning prayer requests, is also mentioned in 9:20 and carried out in the prayer (9:15-19), it becomes possible only as a merciful (9:9,18) product of confession (9:4-14). There is no corresponding mention of prayer requests at the beginning (9:4), so such requests were not viewed as central at that vantage point.

If anything, the sense that confession is the "heart and soul" of this magnificent prayer is heightened by the description in Daniel 9:20. There Daniel reflects back on this just-finished masterpiece of blended order and passion.[4] He first refers to "speaking and praying," but then quickly fine-tunes what he meant as "confessing my sin and the sin of my people Israel." In essence, Daniel is summarizing his prayer in terms like these: "I've been honestly talking to the Lord about the multiplied and prolonged sin of my wider family tree and confessing my direct responsibility for it in the present tense."

In order to make the applicational discussion of Daniel's prayer most helpful, there are two integrally related subjects that need to be further spotlighted. The first is the difficulty of "piercing" denial to bring about confession. The second is the awkward but realistic need to bring your family tree to your time of confession before the Lord.

TRUE CONFESSION AND TENACIOUS DENIAL

One of the most important verses in the entire Bible on confession of sin and forgiveness is 1 John 1:9. Because I teach biblical interpretation, I always seek to pay close attention to the surrounding context of an idea or verse. But until I began to understand biblical recovery, the immediate context of that wonderful promise "to forgive us our sins and to cleanse us from all unrighteousness" in response to heartfelt "confession" didn't make much sense.

Why in the world would the Apostle John place these words—"If we say that we have no sin, we are deceiving ourselves, and the truth is not in us" (1 John 1:8)—just before the great confession and forgiveness verse?[5] Equally puzzling, why would he follow it with "If we say that we have not sinned, we make Him a liar, and His word is not in us" (1:10)? Was John treating his readers like kids, assuming ignorance on their part or beating them over the head with a pet concern of his?

None of the above, though I've come to realize that the correct answer does involve a radical wake-up call. John is not off on a personal crusade to beat everyone into line. But he obviously does think that two crucial points related to the promise in 1 John 1:9 need to be registered forcefully with his readers in order for them fully to comprehend what is involved with confession.

The first of these, found in 1 John 1:8, is *the consistent human tendency to self-deception in regard to sin.* This pattern can helpfully be termed "internal spiritual denial." It is classically evidenced in many churches when, during a time set aside for confession of sin during the service, or before taking the Lord's Supper, we can't think of anything to confess.

Since John is clearly writing to those who are already believers (5:13), it is an invalid "dodge" to claim that Christians aren't sinners. And that seems to be exactly the kind of response John is anticipating when he makes his preemptive strike in 1 John 1:8. The wise veteran apostle is at pains to leave no doubt that, if you think you don't have a sin problem to "recover" from in some meaningful sense, you are lying to yourself. Nothing more and nothing less!

John is also a step ahead of the denying believers in his readership who would attempt to soften the force of his indictment in 1:8. He knows they will back up and retrench with an attitude such as, "Okay, I'll admit I mess up sometimes. But at least I'm not hurting anyone but myself."

Besides all the other nearby human beings who would not even take a deep breath before disagreeing, there is another major flaw in that outlook, according to 1 John 1:10.[6] It overlooks the *most* "Significant Other Person" in the believer's life, the One who is always there for us in a concerned but healthy way.[7]

If there is anyone more spiritually blind and deaf than the self-deception artist in 1 John 1:8, it is the "vertical denial" ego-maniacs who expect to prove that God is a liar (and they are not). These individuals may appear confident on the outside, but on the inside they are so desperately afraid of facing their responsibility for sin that in effect they try to "pass the buck" to the Lord (1:10). Of course it won't work . . . at least not for very long. The Lord and His Word are the embodiment of truth, and the truth *will* come out.

By now you, like me, are probably beginning to admire the Apostle John's realistic insights on redeemed human nature. He knows the wily species amazingly well from many years of ministry-based observation. Above all else, he wants his readers to know that the tendency to deny sin is incredibly strong (1 John 1:8,10). Even the marvelous promise of full forgiveness and spiritual cleansing, if a person will simply own up to the spiritual reality of things (1:9), often hardly makes a dent in the high-gloss shine of denial.

Looking back at his spiritually insensitive ancestors, Daniel would have agreed wholeheartedly with John's "reality theology." What made things worse, though, is that their long-ago-and-far-away sin and denial was still causing Daniel and his people here-and-now problems. Worst of all, these problems, which Daniel had nothing to do with starting, would continue to haunt the future unless Daniel acted decisively to silence the reverberating effects of sin.

CANDID CONFESSIONS OF THE GENOGRAM

Some people are very resistant to the idea that "the sins of the fathers" (Exodus 20:5) can still wreak havoc in the present. I have often heard such well-intentioned souls ask things like, "Isn't that trying to blame someone else who can't defend himself for your problems?"

Sure, some people will try to blame *anyone else* who is convenient, including God. But the actions and decisions of the past will keep flowing through the present like Old Man River until somebody diverts its flow, often at great personal cost.

Try telling the victims of multi-generational alcoholic or child-abusing families, including some in influential roles in evangelical ministries, that the family past does not have any effect on the present. Only those still tightly cocooned in denial will deny that it does.

Perhaps you have come to the point of admitting that the personalities and behavior of your parents, grandparents, and other close family members might be impacting your life and relationships in a negative way. If so, you would be greatly enlightened by constructing an "emotional family tree."

An emotional family tree is constructed in the same way that a genealogical family tree is charted, except that the focus is on emotional-relational data for each person and family instead of bare historical facts.

Putting together such a personal "genogram" is becoming a fairly widespread exercise in counseling. In that setting, it is used much like a doctor uses a patient's personal and family medical history in diagnosing a problem and suggesting appropriate treatment.

This tool is not limited to highly trained professionals. A person who is not an academically qualified historian can do an adequate job on a family genealogical project, why should it be notably different with a genogram?

In order to field-test my conviction on this point, I introduced the genogram approach in a class called "Biblical Exposition of Fatherhood," which I offered at Talbot School of Theology during the spring 1992 term. The course was designed to integrate biblical and contemporary family/societal issues.

I was concerned about student reactions, mostly because of the large size and great diversity of the class. So I played it pretty close to the vest in explaining the genogram concept and applying it to my relationship with my dad and what I know of his relationship with his father.

My fears were unfounded. The concept ignited in that class, and it continued to pop up spontaneously throughout the semester in student questions, sectional round-table discussions, and student papers. The icing on the cake was the high number of students who listed the period given over to the genogram as one highlight of the entire course, which received quite favorable overall evaluations.

Understanding the family origin of certain personality traits and behavioral patterns can be a scary or anger-inducing experience. But it can also help make us realists and even provide hope for changing what blind-sides most people out of the past.

DANIEL'S SHAME-FULL GENOGRAM

Having worked through painful personal background issues, Daniel certainly would not have backed away from the challenge of facing wider family sins. Considering the number of relatively specific titles for various roles in Judah that he employs in 9:6-8, it is not unlikely that Daniel had certain people's names and behavioral patterns in mind as he prayed his great prayer of confession.

For just a moment, imagine what Daniel's self-developed genogram might have been like. His parents, most likely wealthy and aristocratic (see 1:3), had been small children during the evil reign of long-lived

King Manasseh (2 Kings 21). What kinds of negative memories and dysfunctional spiritual models would they have internalized before Josiah's reforms began to take hold (2 Kings 22–23)?

It is also very possible that Daniel's grandparents had to suffer or die at Manasseh's hands earlier in his fifty-five-year reign because of their godliness or to give in to the pervasive idolatry and witchcraft of the time.[8] There is an even more shocking possibility: Daniel could easily have been a member of "the royal family" (Daniel 1:3) and thus directly descended from Manasseh, the most abusive and diabolical king in Judah's history.[9] Not exactly fond or healthy memories!

Maybe you see where I'm headed with this. Until we begin to attach specific names and specific actions to our confession before God—whether personal or in regard to our families—it tends to remain theoretical and distant, not concrete and personal. Naming names (however dreaded) and actions (however hurtful) can be a giant step in the direction of forgiveness and eventual healing.

EGG ON YOUR FACE

In Daniel 9:7-8 the somewhat odd rendering "open shame" means literally "shame of face." This is a graphic word picture of shame that shows (or is spread) all over one's face.

In our culture, we use the similar image of "egg on your face" to make the same point about embarrassing behavior and its visible aftermath. If it helps you follow Daniel's thought patterns as he moves into the body of his prayer, in your mind's eye picture Daniel and a whole host of other Judahites kneeling before the Lord in prayer with "spiritual egg" smeared all over their faces.

To push the analogy a step further, the egg is on the faces of both fully deserving parties and innocent bystanders. Besides those whose sin was worthy of a crate of rotten eggs, others (like Daniel) simply did not know when to duck and got plastered by eggs intended for the truly shameful parties.

So when Daniel gets to the "shame, shame!" part of his prayer, he has included both groups. The "true shame" of the first group is largely deserved because of their shameful and willful acts and longer-term patterns. The second group includes those caught in the backwash of the sin of the first group, as well as many who have been "shamed" by others emotionally but are not directly responsible.

These different kinds of shame continue on to the present day. Shameful actions by some still bring great shame on those whose role in the acts was not direct in any sense. In these cases where shame has hit hard, both the catalysts for shame and the ones who couldn't "duck" its effects, like Daniel, need to prayerfully seek recovery.

ESCALATING LEVELS OF RESPONSIBILITY

Besides this important clarification about types of shame, another helpful distinction can be made regarding the amount of responsibility shouldered by various parties mentioned in Daniel's prayer. After all, Daniel was careful to define what he meant by the plural pronoun *we* in "we have sinned" (9:5).

In Daniel 9:6 we find the categories of "kings," "princes," "fathers," and "all the people of the land." That last phrase seems to be broken up geographically in 9:7: "Judah," "Jerusalem," and "all Israel" (now scattered in consequence of the judgment of Exile). The first three terms are repeated in exactly the same order in 9:8.

Why did Daniel go to such lengths to list these people groups and locations? Sure, he was scrupulously following scriptural guidelines, but the requirement of the Mosaic Law was simply that the people "confess their iniquity and the iniquity of their forefathers" (Leviticus 26:40). Was this just a flight of elegant, but otherwise unpurposeful, rhetoric on Daniel's part?

Let's make a comparison to get some insight into what Daniel was up to. In a hypothetical scenario, the United States slides economically, militarily, and morally into becoming a third-rate nation and is eventually taken over by an emergent "superpower." In the post-mortem evaluations, who would be considered responsible for the "death" of this once-great nation? From one perspective, all citizens would have to be held responsible for standing by and allowing the downfall to occur. Yet the elected national and state leaders, as well as the movers and shakers in business and public policy circles, had the most official authority and clout. Shouldn't they be held accountable for their tragically mistaken decisions and policies?

There seems no way around the conclusion that every citizen is responsible *to some degree*. Likewise, there seems to be no denying that the leaders in the various fields are responsible *to a greater degree.*

This same reasoning also applies at the focal point of most recovery issues: the family. The concept of codependency has rightly observed that everyone in a family unit either actively or passively "enables" the addict or abusive personality to get away with abusive patterns over time. Yet it is plain to see that the actual perpetrator is most directly responsible. Next in line, it seems clear that the head of the household bears much of the responsibility.

In his ordered listing of "kings," "princes," and "fathers" (perhaps meaning both tribal and family heads) in 9:6 and 9:8, Daniel leaves the clear implication that those occupying such roles were indeed more responsible for Judah's demise than "all the people of the land" (9:6). It is also possible, though less clear, that some pattern of concentric (geographical) circles of responsibility can be inferred from 9:7, starting with the royal palace and the Temple in Jerusalem and working outward.

The bottom line here for recovery application is that no one involved in such a dysfunctional setting can legitimately claim "I'm not responsible." The situation can be fully rectified only if everyone involved is willing to be a responsible person.

On the other hand, neither can the person who is the catalyst for the dysfunctional behavior or abuse merely sink back into the group and refuse to own the brunt of the responsibility. The decisions and actions that set the whole painful situation in motion were made by that person. That must be made unmistakably clear if there is to be real hope of healing and change.

THE LORD WHO BALANCES FORGIVENESS
AND ACCOUNTABILITY

Having assigned precise responsibility for the mess the Jews had gotten themselves into nearly seventy years earlier, Daniel, the recovery prayer-warrior, turns again to consider the perfect character and resources of "the Lord our God" (9:9). The contrast between undeserving "shame on the face" humanity and sinless, yet compassionate and forgiving, Divinity is stark and undoubtedly purposeful. The truism "To err is human, to forgive is divine" is certainly valid in regard to Daniel's great prayer for recovery.

Still, as forgiving as the Lord truly is, that one fabulous quality must not be universalized in our minds as the totality of His character. Too many people latch on to a single quality such as forgiveness, then expand it until they see God simply as the cosmic Forgiver . . . and nothing else. Although most people with deep-seated recovery issues have exactly the opposite perspective—great difficulty receiving God's forgiveness—some other dysfunctional personalities presume mightily on the Lord forgiving and forgiving and forgiving again . . . with no true repentance on their part.

Even though Daniel clings to God's forgiveness for dear life (9:9), he is under no illusion that the Lord is a monotone Personality. No sooner has Daniel referred to the forgiveness factor than he balances it with the accountability that the Lord requires from His creatures (9:10).

Daniel is quite clear on the obedience that God expects. He makes no excuses for his people's ongoing disregard of the Lord's scriptural standards or refusal to listen to the prophets God sent to call them back to biblical truth and behavior. God desires to forgive them, but He will not simply look the other way when they flaunt His scriptural boundaries. People with recovery needs will do well to imitate Daniel's "balancing act" so that they neither overestimate nor underestimate the forgiveness of the Lord of recovery.

THE OPPOSITE OF A CHARMED LIFE

Think of those few wonderful times in life when everything goes just right. Every decision turns out to be correct. Everything you touch turns to gold. You are definitely on a roll. (You might even make a few five-foot putts along the way!) But inevitably, at some point the roll stops rolling. The Midas Touch loses it sheen, and the luster of the "charmed life" turns plain and dull.

This is basically what happened to the Jewish people, though it did not occur overnight. And the change was not due to a quirky change in fortune. The connection was clear: When they had obeyed God's Law, they had been greatly blessed by the Lord (Deuteronomy 28:1-14). When widespread disobedience began to dominate their culture (Daniel 9:10), the refreshing breezes of God's provision began to heat up into a tortuous "curse" (9:11; see Deuteronomy 28:15-68).

I have sometimes wondered in the last five years, my period of residency in Southern California, whether the Lord is heating up some sort of "curse" on this part of the country. Over that period of time, we have gone from the frying pan of a major drought and colossal traffic and economic problems into the literal fire of the 1992 Los Angeles riots.

Of course, sunny Southern California is not the nation of Israel under the direct covenant stipulations of the Mosaic Law. So on one level, this is an apples-and-oranges comparison. Yet if disobedience to God's clearly stated behavioral standards were the only basis for the curse, unquestionably this "do your own thing" subculture would be due for a divine blast-job. If that were to happen, it is difficult to know whether the bulk of the teeming millions in this vast megalopolis would be any more open to confession and repentance than their ancient Jewish counterparts.

Regardless of whether we can answer how the Lord may or may not deal with the sin of nations, urban areas, or people groups today, there is no confusion over how He disciplines His individual children. Perhaps the clearest biblical passage on this subject is Hebrews 12:

> God deals with you as with sons; for what son is there whom his father does not discipline? But if you are without discipline, of which all have become partakers, then you are illegitimate children and not sons. . . . All discipline for the moment seems not to be joyful, but sorrowful; yet to those who have been trained by it, afterwards it yields the peaceful fruit of righteousness. (verses 7-8,11)

This passage makes it clear that God disciplines (or even temporarily "curses") His people as a loving Father would a rebellious child. He takes no pleasure in their pain, but the training is necessary to move them in the righteous and fruitful direction He wants them to go.

If you are going through a tough time in your Christian walk or in regard to recovery issues, take heart. The Lord doesn't have it in for you! He treats all His sons and daughters that way when they get outside the bounds He has set for them.

In fact, God has sworn a binding "oath" (Daniel 9:11) that He will deal with perfect fatherly firmness toward His sinning children. In the process, He's simply turning up the heat to get your attention and cooperation in the biblical recovery process, much as He did with the Jews of the Exile in Daniel's day.

SPIRITUAL HIROSHIMA AFTER THE BOMB

What would it have been like to witness the terrible transformation of the city of Hiroshima, Japan, into a deadly burned-out crater? Would there have been any hope for that once-proud city in the wake of the atomic bomb catastrophe? Those and similar questions have come to mind more than once in recent years in my acquaintance with Japanese students at Talbot School of Theology.

Frankly, I loathe the uneasiness and stab of pain that I feel when I even ask such questions. Nearly fifty years later, the circumstances and horror of that destruction still pack an emotional knockout punch—even for someone like me, who has never been any closer to Hiroshima than a picture in an encyclopedia or an image on television.

Would it have been much different emotionally for Daniel as he recalled the "great calamity" that had befallen Jerusalem? He was not there to see it happen any more than I was in Hiroshima. But Daniel had heard the monstrous details, and they had been stored away inside him for almost fifty years at this point.[10] He knew only too well that "under the whole heaven there has not been done anything like what was done to Jerusalem" (Daniel 9:12).

As Daniel rewound his thinking to survey the devastating consequences of Judah's sin (9:11-12), he undoubtedly felt very deeply some of his own personal pain and loss. That is true of anyone who suffers a monumental setback, even if it is indirect—for example, of a huge corporate variety. There is still your emotional "slice of the pie" to have to work through. It doesn't matter whether you are a very healthy personality or someone with a serious recovery profile—except that it's considerably harder for those needing recovery to face the reality of such painful consequences and personal loss.

Daniel faced up to the reality honestly and thoroughly, and so can you and I. Do you feel as if there's no hope to rebuild your life? That's what the average observer thought of the pathetic ruins almost fifty years after Jerusalem's "calamity." But, as we will see, that is not what the Lord had in mind for Jerusalem.[11]

It is also not what God has in mind for you or me. If recovery can spring up out of a big pile of Judean rubble, you and I can certainly emerge from under the painful piles of devastation in our lives through the Lord's power for restoration.

FINDING THE MISSING LINK

For many years, scientists in fields such as paleontology and geology have been engaged in a frantic search to find "the missing link," a definitive piece of evidence that will cement the theory of evolution as fact. In spite of some ballyhooed instances, which later proved to be incredibly overstated or out-and-out trumped up, such proof is still lacking. And I, for one, will not hold my breath waiting for such a missing link to make its appearance.

Daniel did not even have to take a deep breath in anticipation of the "missing link" in the relationship between God and His people. It's very simple: *repentance*. The word is not used in Daniel 9:13. But the concept is written all over the last half of that verse.

The term *repentance* means, basically, a change of mind, though the emotional and behavioral "fruits in keeping with repentance" (Luke 3:8) must follow in order for full biblical repentance to take hold.[12] Those "fruits" are what Daniel is talking about in the phrase "turning from our iniquity and giving attention to Thy truth" (Daniel 9:13).

Daniel is essentially admitting to the Lord: "We haven't done the simplest and most obvious thing to recultivate Your favor. As a wider group of people, we haven't even decisively broken from our sin in repentance, nor sought guidance from Your biblical truth." No wonder God was still sternly "frowning" on His strayed people, as the picturesque Hebrew language behind the rendering "sought the favor" (9:13) suggests.

But the Lord is more than willing to start "smiling" at His people again at any point. All He asks of us in seeking to regain His favor is that we respect His biblical boundaries and standards. They are there for good reasons and for our own good.

When we fall flat on our faces in sin or dysfunctional behavior, He is ready, willing, and able to help us dust off and get moving forward again, basking in the warmth of His smile. The only obstructing factor is a prideful lack of repentance on the part of the person who has fallen and desperately needs recovery. That is the missing link that too many hurting people, even believers, never find because they are looking for relief in all the wrong places.

5

BACK TO THE FUTURE, BIBLICALLY

Because of home video, I eventually get to view some movies that I wouldn't necessarily take the time to go out to see. In this way I was able to see all three *Back to the Future* movies on the home discount plan.

Though I do not at all wish to endorse that trio of movies in every detail, their basic premise is interesting to consider as we continue our study of Daniel's "Prayer for Recovery." From these two widely divergent contexts, the same basic principle emerges: *The present is shaped by past actions, and a better future can be reshaped by present actions.*

In each installment of *Back to the Future,* Marty (Michael J. Fox) and Doc (Christopher Lloyd) take Doc's super-charged DeLorean time machine into past and future dimensions. There are comical, but thought-provoking, insights regarding the ongoing impact of the past on the present and the need to act responsibly in the present in order to right the course of the future.

PAST CHOICES AND THE PRESENT

As problems popped up in the town of Hill Valley in 1985, Marty and Doc repeatedly traveled back to various points in the past to attempt to untangle the mess before it could begin to congeal in 1985. They always chose to go directly to the root cause and nip it in the bud.

71

They were practicing what might be called "preemptive intervention." If only such a thing could be done in real life to preempt the traumas that spawn recovery issues!

Daniel, by contrast, could not mount a preemptive strike on the past problems he was facing. His only recourse in relation to the past was to disarm the present-tense impact device that had begun ticking when Israel had turned away from the Lord in sin.

Daniel had begun this defusing mission with in-depth Bible study and the application of heartfelt mourning over "the sins of the fathers" (Exodus 20:5), as we can see in Daniel 9:2-3. As he began his prayer, Daniel brought the ever-faithful Lord (9:4) together with himself, the one willing to stand responsible for the sins of his unfaithful forefathers (9:5-6).[1] In doing so, Daniel anticipated the marvelous offer made by the writer of Hebrews: "Let us therefore draw near with confidence to the throne of grace, that we may receive mercy and may find grace to help in time of need" (4:16).

What a wonderful example for those with painful recovery issues! Daniel models the responsibility they must assume for the actions that got them into their dysfunctional situation. And he illustrates their need for grace in abundance as they shoulder that responsibility!

The prayer gathers momentum as Daniel accurately confesses the ongoing shameful behavior and disobedience of his forefathers (9:7-10). Because of these past acts of rebellion against the Lord, there would be no hope for the exiled people of Judah if it were not for the compassion and forgiveness of their trustworthy God. But there is hope for both the Jews in Daniel's day and believers with heavy emotional baggage because God's compassion and forgiveness are available in generous portions for His hurting children.

Through the heart of his great recovery prayer (9:11-13), Daniel chooses to live in the real world. He faces the heartbreaking reality of the curse his people were under related to the Mosaic Law, which took the form of unparalleled catastrophe that the Lord had rained out on Jerusalem. It is extremely difficult for later descendants who have risen above the behavior of the "black sheep" of generations gone by, as Daniel certainly had, to come to terms with the reality that the present branches of the family still are connected to and affected by the family "roots."

Short of being able to venture back into the past, Daniel did as much as he could to cut loose from the devastating effects of sinful past actions. While he could not alter the present he had inherited, he could very much make a difference in the future by disengaging from the sinful web of the past. He could begin praying and living in such a way that the restoration could be worked out in the time ahead.

PRESENT CHOICES AND THE FUTURE

The second *Back to the Future* film shifts the focus from the impact of past actions in the present to the impact of present actions on the future. In the process, the intertwining of past, present, and future generations of Marty's family occasionally gets eerie in spite of the rapid-fire action and humor.

Daniel's prayer also begins to prepare to shift gears from a primarily past-present focus to a present-future one starting in 9:14-15. But it does not leave the past until the need related to Jerusalem's calamity is recalled once more (9:14) alongside the compelling illustration of the Jewish people's restoration from Egypt at the time of the Exodus (9:15).

It is very healthy to be able to face up to the pain of the past while simultaneously recalling positive memories. This "separating nuggets and slag" strategy allows a person in recovery to face the negative side of life honestly without letting it crowd out the true joy of positive memories.

Only in Daniel 9:16-19 does the recovery prayer warrior proceed to making requests of the Lord. The blend of passionate appeal for the Lord to hear and bold supplication is amazingly personal! Daniel tugs at the Lord's sleeve as a beloved child would in making request of a father he knows will hear him out.

This sort of intimate prayer is difficult to understand for people who have been held at an emotional arm's length throughout life. But as their recovery proceeds, they can develop this kind of closeness to the Lord, even as they can learn to experience true intimacy with other people. That is how present-tense choices and experiences can build, one step at a time, into a much better future.

WAITING TO DUMP THE LOAD

One of the few movies I did go out to see last year was a well-done—though not necessarily well-known—film called *Memphis Belle,* focusing on the lives of a crew on a World War II bomber.

In that movie, there was a tension-filled climactic scene that vividly reminds me of the first part of Daniel 9:14. The "Belle" was deep over German territory on the way to dump its payload of bombs on its high-priority target. The air was thick with anti-aircraft flak. Damage to the plane and injuries to the crew made it seem unlikely that they could ever make it all the way to the target.

But the crew stuck with it and finally dropped their bombs at just the precise instant, completely destroying their target. The movie wasn't over then, however. They had successfully completed their bombing mission, but they still had to get home in one piece. Then, and only then, could everyone heave a collective sigh of relief.

The story line of *Memphis Belle* is actually quite similar to the way the Lord brought the calamity of judgment on the people of Judah, particularly on Jerusalem. Though no amount of earthly "flak" could have stopped God's stated mission of judgment, the delayed timing and final completion aspects operated in surprisingly parallel ways.

The Hebrew construction of the first part of Daniel 9:14 makes it clear that the great judgment that Judah sustained had been ready and waiting for the right time to "drop the payload."[2] God acted at exactly the right moment in history to make the biggest impact, and not just for the sake of His just judgment. The Jews, like a person doggedly denying the need for recovery, had to "hit bottom" with a resounding thud before they could take the first steps toward their eventual renewal.

From the prophecies in Jeremiah 25 and 29 that Daniel had studied as background for this prayer, it is clear that the Lord never had any intention of climaxing the mission by "bombing" Jerusalem.[3] Instead, like the return of the Memphis Belle, Judah would be brought back "in one piece" to begin its collective recovery process in the Promised Land. Only then would God's "tough love" toward Judah, focused particularly in the Babylonian Exile, bring the action to the culminating stage of "mission accomplished."

THE ONLY "TOTALLY RIGHTEOUS" ONE

As a small child, I was afflicted with a bad case of the "Why?"'s. As long as I can remember, I have been at least as fascinated with *why* things are the way they are as with *what* they are.

This native curiosity did not endear me to my career-military father, who took every "Why?" as a sign of insubordination. However, Dad did not succeed in stamping out my nagging curiosity; he merely drove it underground. I'm happy to say that over the years—particularly through my recovery process—it has made its way back up from the subterranean caverns of my personality to be "alive and well" as a major stimulus for my research, teaching, preaching, and writing.

Of course, I must admit that not all of my curiosity has redeeming social value. For example, I have wondered for over twenty-five years why Bill Medley and Bobby Hatfield called themselves "The Righteous Brothers." That particular "why" popped up again when the California youth vocabulary offered "Totally righteous, dude!" as another of its gifts for language-enrichment.

There are parts of this tomfoolery, however, that have serious implications for the description of the Lord's personality and motivation in Daniel 9:14. When He is described there as "righteous in respect to all deeds," I read that as "totally" righteous, especially when the other references to God's righteousness in Daniel's prayer (9:7,16) are taken into account. The Lord is the only "Dude" who can lay legitimate claim to being "totally righteous." Also, because everything He does is always right, we cannot lay blame on Him. Instead, we must accept the responsibility for our own actions—or, if someone else caused the damage and dysfunction, the responsibility to begin the restoration process.

POSITIVE MEMORIES

Excuse me for another brief spasm of musical nostalgia, but who could ever forget the Lettermen's great hit song "Memories"? Even in the painful times of my growing-up years, that song could lift my spirits.

Some people have been so constantly abused in their lives that there are virtually no positive memories for them to draw on for comfort and hope as they begin recovery. However, most people do have a fund of positive, perhaps even happy, memories they can cling to along the pathway of recovery. It may be that, like me, you have to unearth memories that have been buried for a long time. But chances are good that it's possible to do so with a prayerful willingness to face whatever is there when you unlock the vault of your memories.

In beginning 9:15, Daniel draws upon a wonderful but distant collective memory for God's people: the Exodus from Egypt, which had occurred some nine centuries in the past.[4] Certainly Daniel does not need to remind the Lord about His mercy shown in bringing Israel out of Egypt. In fact, the Lord had stated in Leviticus 26:45 how His "memories" would function in restoring His people to the Promised Land.[5]

So why does Daniel bring up the Exodus at this point? Probably for two reasons: (1) To maximize the "common ground" with the Lord over this serious topic for prayer; and (2) to encourage himself in regard to God's powerful Person and "personal-touch" power (9:15).

Understanding "common ground" is also very important in strengthening the relational part of any recovery. Without denying the problems or differences, it is necessary to get each person who is facing the particular recovery needs squarely on the same team. The recovery of the Exodus meant that God and Daniel were in complete agreement that another recovery could happen because that's the way He deals with His people. They were not at odds; they were teammates working toward the goal of restoration.

The factor of personal encouragement is always a huge need in the recovery process. People from dysfunctional or abusive backgrounds are almost always discouraged and many times deeply depressed. Their home on the range was a place where seldom was heard an *encouraging* word. Consequently, any encouraging sign, event, or word is a breath of fresh air amid the blood, sweat, and tears of recovery.

THE GREATEST MARQUEE NAME

Because of the outrageous amounts of money being paid actors and professional athletes today, the "entertainment" industry is trying more and more to secure its profits by focusing on so-called marquee names. These are the ultimately marketable figures, such as Kevin Costner or Michael Jordan, who seem to draw huge throngs to anything that involves them.

This sort of crass commercialism, which plays on some of the basest idolatrous instincts in sinful human nature, normally turns me off to the max. Recently, though, an unlikely marquee name drew a massive crowd that was deserved and appropriate.

The California Angels baseball team recently retired the number of Nolan Ryan, who pitched for the Angels from 1971–1979. In a season when Angels' victories have been few and far between, attendance has been poor. But Ryan's retirement bash drew over fifty-one thousand fans to Anaheim Stadium. Then, when the ageless Ryan pitched for the visiting Texas Rangers the next night, at least thirty-two thousand came to cheer him on. Announcers and sports writers all agreed that hardly anyone was rooting for the Angels that night in their home stadium.

The most amazing thing about Nolan Ryan is that he has outlasted so many other marquee names. In fact, he was let go by two teams he had played for at length, California and the Houston Astros, because he was considered over the hill—too old to keep throwing that ninety-five-mile-per-hour fastball and wicked curveball. Many strikeout records and no-hit games later, he continues to defy the odds and serve as a fabulous "attendance-enhancer" wherever he pitches.

As great as Nolan Ryan is as a person and pitcher, he is but a faint illustration of the greatest ageless marquee name of all: the Lord God Himself. In Daniel 9:15 the great prophet, himself something of a marquee name, says to the Lord in no uncertain terms, "You have made the biggest-league Name for Yourself, and You are still *the* all-time marquee name."[6]

Let's track with Daniel's thought at this point. He seems to be saying that God earned a "big name" in the eyes of the world at large by powerfully bringing Israel out of Egypt (9:15). That part is fairly obvious. "As it is this day" (9:15) agrees that the Lord still deserves His "big name." But, and very important to the rest of the prayer, God's infinitely good Name is being called into question because of the shameful status of His people and the site of His Temple, Jerusalem (9:16-19).

Although Daniel is undoubtedly reasoning with the Lord to get Him to act to vindicate His good Name (9:19), there may be an additional recovery-related factor at work. Daniel is admitting that, as compassionate and forgiving as God is (9:9,18-19), the people of Judah have still been an embarrassment to *Him* (9:15). Coming to terms with shame (9:7-8) and the reality of that embarrassment are giant steps in the direction of recovery.

A SINFUL CITY IN THE HANDS OF AN ANGRY GOD

Perhaps the most well-known sermon to come out of the widespread revival known as the Great Awakening in colonial New England was Jonathan Edwards' "Sinners in the Hands of an Angry God." Admittedly, it was an amazingly vivid and compelling message. However, the disproportionate amount of attention paid to that one sermon about God's righteous judgment has greatly muddied the water in evaluating Edwards and the rest of his ministry.

It is probably not too much to say that Jonathan Edwards was among the handful of greatest minds during the American Colonial Period. It is also fair to say that the subject and tone of the famous "Sinners" message was relatively rare over the span of Edwards' ministry. Thus the widespread misconception that Jonathan Edwards was merely a fire-breathing evangelist is an extremely unfair blight on Edwards' name.

Daniel seems to have a similar concern about God's Name when he brings up the devastation and reproach of Jerusalem and the people of Judah in 9:16. Daniel is upset because, as he says, "all those around us" think the worst about the situation. All that the surrounding nations of that day saw was God's "anger" and "wrath" lying heavily on the rubble that had been Jerusalem, the Lord's "holy mountain" (9:16).

From this unfortunate limited exposure, many would conclude that Judah's God was all wrath and judgment. Daniel knew much better, and he would momentarily begin his appeal to the compassion and forgiveness of the Lord. But he wanted all the onlookers to see the whole, balanced "package" of God's personality.

Daniel's concern is no less important for believers with dysfunctional or abusive backgrounds. In projecting an image upon God from their faulty, derived understanding of a "father figure," such wounded individuals rarely get emotionally close to a full-orbed view of the Lord's perfectly balanced personality. In their attempts to understand a heavenly Father, they get stuck in the rut of their "shaping relationship" with a human father. But as Daniel 9:16 implies, that faulty understanding can be reshaped as we become increasingly familiar (intellectually *and* emotionally) with the riches of the personality of the God of grace and truth.

ABOVE REPROACH?

The basic overall requirement for being an elder in the Church of Jesus Christ is to be "above reproach" in reputation and behavior (1 Timothy 3:2, Titus 1:6). This blamelessness is very important because of the way a leader's name in the community can reflect on the reputation of the entire church and even the Lord.[7]

After having worked throughout his career in foreign secular governments (Daniel 1:19-21), Daniel was keenly aware of the bad reputation cast on both Judah and Jerusalem by the Babylonian Exile (9:16). Although the behavior of God's people had hardly been "above reproach," Daniel feared that the reproach would spread. He reasoned, "Thy city and Thy people are called by Thy name" (9:19). Since the Jews had "stunk up the place" through their prolonged sin and disastrous judgment, Daniel did not want the "stink" to spread to God's spotless and blameless reputation.

This is an important point to consider in regard to recovery. Many believers, especially leaders, invest years in establishing a reputation that is "above reproach." But men and women who labor earnestly to establish a strong testimony for the Lord are not immune to an unanticipated volcanic eruption of deeply buried trauma or other pain.

Since it is entirely realistic to be a committed Christian and still have to wrestle with recovery issues somewhere along the way, we must try to think through in advance the possible need for "blameless damage control." By that I mean how to handle things with true wisdom and discretion if you, or one close to you, get(s) blind-sided by recovery pain.

Even more important, of course, is the prior determination to face the issues responsibly, not using the confusion and pain as any sort of an excuse for "going over the edge" morally or otherwise.[8] As godly as he was in many ways, David's inability to stop himself from going over the edge in his affair with Bathsheba left scars on his reputation and family for the rest of his life (and beyond).

Disturbingly, it is often the believers who blindly and naively insist "That can't happen to me!" who end up trying to salvage their wrecked lives after a crash. Sadly, many such testimony-killers could have been averted with a little less pride, a little more honesty, and some wise and prayerful recovery-planning.

SUNSHINE IN THE RAIN

I think it's time that I come out of the closet in making another embarrassing personal revelation: I like happy faces. I don't mean the clownlike smiles that people put on to try to paint over internal frowns or tears. I mean the ones that are printed on those little buttons people wear or scrawled on letters and school papers.

In case you're wondering, I don't draw happy faces on my students' papers (although I like it when a happy face greets me from their papers). But the prophet Daniel had no such reservations about asking God to put on a "happy face" for His people. He prayed unashamedly, "O Lord, let Thy face shine on Thy desolate sanctuary" (9:17). That's boils down to, "Lord, *smile* at Your demolished Temple."[9]

If God is happy with His people, things are definitely headed in the right direction. The Lord will not be a hypocrite and smile just to be pleasant. His face will shine only when He is satisfied that His standards are being met.

As I have worked through my own recovery, I have deeply desired a fatherly smile from time to time. It helps me to think of those times when my dad smiled at me. It also helps when I think of Daniel 9:17 and the Lord's shining face, like a burst of sunshine breaking through the rain and cloud cover.

STOP, LOOK, AND LISTEN

When I was a kid, we were taught to stop, look, and listen at every corner, crosswalk, train crossing—you name it. To a know-it-all kid (which more of us were than we would like to admit), that kind of training is boring if not frustrating. But you have to see only one fatality because somebody didn't stop, look, and listen to realize that it's not overkill. It's learning to be thorough, to be safe, to be tuned in to all the related things going on around you.

In a very real sense, Daniel is imploring God to do something similar in 9:18. Having already asked Him to "stop" being angry with His people, Daniel now passionately entreats the Lord to "listen" and "look" at the desolate remains of the city of Jerusalem and the desperate remnant of the people of Judah. He does so because the safety and future of many people is at stake at this "crossroads" of history.

From a recovery standpoint, this "stop, look, and listen" principle applies both to ourselves and to our relationship with the Lord. To stop, look, and listen is to evaluate your life honestly, including listening carefully to other people who care about you but will also speak the truth in love. You may be deep in denial with almost no clue, as I was.

You can also rest assured that God will stop, look, and listen when you ask Him to, even as He did with Daniel. He is a Father who is never too busy to stop what He's doing, look you in the eye, and listen carefully when you reveal to Him what's on your heart.

FORGIVE . . . WITHOUT DELAY!

It is now well-established that grief is a process. It is also becoming widely accepted that in many cases, forgiveness is also a process. That should not be a major shock, considering that the emotional dynamics of forgiveness are often amazingly similar to grief.

I will confess that I have not always looked at things this way. For a long time I thought and taught that forgiveness was a simple, point-in-time "business transaction" essentially devoid of emotional content. Somehow I got away with that nonsense for years . . . until I ran into a personal situation where it took me two years to forgive a fellow believer fully.

This person had done everything in his power to nail me because I had called his bluff as a church power-broker. He never got within a hundred miles of asking my forgiveness for the diabolical things he said behind my back and repeatedly tried to do.

So what did I do, great spiritual giant that I was? Did I model after the Savior on the cross and say, "Father, forgive him; for he doesn't know what he's doing"? Guess again.

I got angrier and angrier with every maneuver he tried. Somehow I couldn't see that my increasing bitterness and unforgiving spirit was really lowering me to his level. Besides that, as in other recovery issues, my lack of forgiveness was sapping much of the energy I needed to face the rest of my relationships and responsibilities.

Having waited the seventy years of the Babylonian Exile for someone to ask forgiveness for the mountain of sins the Jewish people had committed, the Lord readily grants His forgiveness when Daniel wholeheartedly asks for it (9:19).[10] But God is perfect, and we are not. Since forgiveness is often a long and difficult process, we must not delay one instant longer than necessary to see that the course of forgiveness is really a bike path running alongside the wider road to recovery.

When you have progressed to the stage of honestly facing the issues related to forgiveness, you are covering some mileage on the road to recovery. You are also headed back to the future—the future to which the Lord is calling you in a biblical, renewing way.[11]

CHAPTER

6

ANOTHER CHANCE
... THANK GOD!

Does a person who has failed deserve a second chance? In perhaps the classic biblical disagreement over this question, Barnabas said yes to the calculated risk of giving John Mark another opportunity after he bailed out on the first missionary journey. Paul's position, however, was an unyielding *no*. He apparently had no intention of running the risk of being left in the lurch by Mark again. As a result of this massive difference of opinion, two great friends and partners went their separate ways, never to join forces directly in ministry again.[1]

Who was right? Was it worth it for either Paul or Barnabas to take this kind of costly stand?

These are not easy questions to answer. But it's worth a try, because at the heart of the dispute was a hurting, embarrassed believer named Mark who was asking for another chance. Mark was wrestling with many of the same recovery issues that trouble us today.

So who was right in this painful face-off? If you use the approach of "Fool me once, shame on you; fool me twice, shame on me," Paul gets the nod. After all, he wanted to prevent the recurrence of a problem that could jeopardize the spread of the gospel. Who can criticize Paul's desire to stabilize his missionary team in preparation for the hardships and dangers they would surely face along the way?

However, this single-minded task orientation is not the only criterion for judging the tug-of-war over Mark. In many cases, it is valid to be a "people person" in the short run while still pursuing the longer-term goal of completing the task. That is precisely what Barnabas was attempting to accomplish with Mark. Beyond this risky salvage operation, he was still fully committed to fulfilling the Great Commission to make disciples of all the nations.[2]

Why did Barnabas undertake such a calculated risk in putting his own wonderful reputation on the line as collateral for Mark? Because he saw the teachableness in Mark's sincere regret of what had happened on the first missionary journey. And because he saw the tremendous potential in Mark's life. Between those two important factors, Barnabas was convinced that he could have his cake (encourage a despairing Mark) and eat it too (receive help from a recovering Mark in effective ministry).

Based on the above reasoning, a very viable case can be made for the rightness of both Paul's position and Barnabas' position. Maybe the question of a second chance should be pronounced an even draw.

But there's a bigger picture to look at here. Let's back away from the dispute itself far enough to ask, "Was it worth it?" Through this wide-angle lens, we can begin to see a very different view.

A WIDER PERSPECTIVE ON THE SECOND CHANCE

In the minds of many students of Scripture, Barnabas is hailed as the classic "encourager" (Acts 4:36) in the New Testament, which is certainly saying a lot in an area that is sorely lacking in many quarters today. Barnabas does not usually receive anywhere near his just due, however, for being a formidable force in wider ministry.

Think about it for a moment. Barnabas is one of those rare individuals who was able to look sensitively and caringly into the eyes of a hurting fellow believer while keeping the big picture clearly in focus. He invested shrewdly in the lives of people, with both high short-term yields *and* long-term cumulative gains.

Let's take a brief run through what we know of Barnabas' life and ministry. When we first encounter him, he is making a magnanimous gift to meet needs in the rapidly expanding Jerusalem church (Acts 4:32-37). But, far from an aloof philanthropist, Barnabas later distinguishes himself by encouraging the struggling new church in Syrian Antioch (11:22-23). His short-term emotional support fueled the longer-term outcome: "considerable numbers were brought to the Lord" (11:24).[3]

That marvelous spiritual harvest in Antioch falls between Barnabas' initial and ongoing relational periods with Paul. Considering what happened in those instances, there is great irony in Paul's outright rejection of a second chance for Mark.

When Paul returned to Jerusalem for the first time after his conversion on the Damascus Road, Barnabas was initially the only one who gave him a chance. Everyone else was too afraid of Paul's former background as a persecutor of the church to be willing even to be seen with Paul. Though Paul proved very effective in Jerusalem after Barnabas' sponsorship broke the ice, he was also controversial and in danger. So, in order to protect Paul and to restore the former peace, the church sent Paul to Tarsus.[4]

It was from Tarsus that Barnabas brought Paul to Antioch (Acts 11:25-26). He was essentially giving him yet "another chance" at the same time that he was developing the effectiveness of the cutting-edge Gentile-oriented ministry in that great city (9:20-21).[5]

Paul's subsequent success in Antioch and on his missionary journeys more than vindicated the calculated risk that Barnabas had "invested" in him. Mark's staying power and effectiveness in the time following Barnabas' decision also proved him right. In addition, it fully persuaded Paul that Mark really was, in the apostle's own words, "useful to me for service."[6]

Who was right about giving Mark another chance? If you take the nearsighted view, it appears that either Paul had the better argument or it was a toss-up. But 20/20 hindsight reveals that Barnabas actually had a better grip on the big picture linking past, present, and future.

That also answers the second question of whether the risk was worth it. Barnabas' decision proved worth the risk many times over in following years, even for Paul—not to mention the incalculable profit to the Church over the ensuing centuries from the Gospel of Mark.[7]

What would have happened if Barnabas hadn't gone out on a limb to recover the fallen Mark? We can thank God that we don't even have to try to answer *that* question.

HOW MANY CHANCES IS ENOUGH?

Before we go blithely on our way, however, there is a very important related question that we need to address: What if a second chance is extended and the wipe-out occurs again—how many more times should another chance be given?

There are two important sides to this coin. One has to do with the mercy of forgiveness, the point we concluded with in the preceding chapter. The other is the factor of accountability—the realistic need not simply to declare that the fallen person is responsible, but to hold that person's feet to the fire or let the consequences teach them what they wouldn't learn otherwise.

In my studied estimation, the classic (and also rather humorous) biblical passage on forgiveness is Matthew 18:21-35. It consists of Peter's question about forgiveness, then Jesus' direct answer and the lengthy parable that illustrates it.

The passage starts with Peter in the process of reaching around to pat himself on the back. When he asks Jesus how many times he should forgive someone's sin against him, Peter doesn't even stop to let Jesus respond. Rather, he plugs in his own magnanimous answer.

If Peter had been asking this question of the Jewish rabbis of his day, he would indeed have come off as a generous man. His offered limit of forgiving seven times is considerably higher than the rabbis' stated limit of three.[8]

But Jesus did not want *any* limit. By stating that we should forgive "up to seventy times seven," Jesus declared "open season" on forgiveness.[9] By employing multiples of seven, the biblical number of completeness, Jesus was sending the message that you can *never* forgive too much.

The parable that follows addresses the corresponding question, "What if you don't forgive?" The bottom line is that a person who will not *extend* the mercy of forgiveness does not deserve to *receive* mercy and forgiveness. That is especially true when we realize that the Lord has forgiven us much more than we will ever have to forgive even the most abusive person.

This parable has a concluding twist that is related to recovery issues (18:35). Christ not only closes the parable by commanding believers to pursue forgiveness, but He also stipulates that the forgiving must be heartfelt. This means that the greater *quantity* of forgiving cannot be allowed in any way to undermine the *quality* of forgiveness. But even more foundationally, it means that Christ defines forgiveness according to what flows from the depths of a person's being, not just as saying the right words or making a mental decision.

Wow! No wonder so many of the people who are clinging to denial for dear life are very unforgiving. If they are out of touch with the issues of the heart, they simply are not able to reach down into the depths of themselves in order to forgive from the heart.

THE BACKBONE OF FORGIVENESS

Forgiveness is one side of the coin. Let's flip it over and look at the other: *accountability*.

As I write these words, memories are still fresh of Steve Howe's latest suspension from baseball for cocaine abuse, classifying him as a "seven-time loser" to drugs.

It was only a year or so earlier that Howe began yet another come-back, but this one was supposed to be different. He claimed to have made a profession of faith in Jesus Christ since his last wipe-out. Along with many others, I wanted to believe and trust Steve Howe. I wanted to see his strong left arm back in baseball. I was rooting for him to "recover" . . . and I still am.

But now he has been caught dead to rights buying cocaine again. What happened? The problem was definitely not lack of forgiveness or the need for another chance. It was lack of accountability.

Where there is no accountability, there probably will not be much recovery. Without clear boundaries and limits, it is altogether too easy to wander out of bounds into a self-indulgent or self-destructive lifestyle.

The book of Judges offers Samson as a classic example of the effects of a lack of accountability, resulting in both self-indulgence and self-destruction.[10] He did not learn until it was too late. What a pity that a life full of such God-given ability would end up in such an embarrassing shambles because no one had the care and courage that added up to speaking the truth in love!

WHAT WAS DANIEL ASKING FOR?

We have already explored Daniel's incredible "Prayer for Recovery" in its original context and as it applies to contemporary issues. The bulk of that intimate communication with the God of righteousness and compassionate forgiveness is the confession of "the sins of the fathers." Having finally come to terms with the past, Daniel concludes the prayer with a passionate plea for the future "recovery" of Judah and Jerusalem.

This is the flow of the prayer in overview, but what was the heart of this meeting with the Lord? What was Daniel foundationally seeking to accomplish by going before God at this point and in this way?

I think Daniel was simply asking for *another chance*. Certainly his fasting, sackcloth, and ashes demonstrated earnest grief about the previous events, but the prophet had no intention of being stuck in the past. Daniel's confession of the prolonged and shameful sin of his people was the primary focus of the prayer, but it was not its climax. Daniel had to get all the cards out on the table before he could finally look the Lord in the eye and request, in effect, "Please forgive us and let us have one more chance to be Your people back in the Promised Land!"

I'm well aware that some practical souls might respond: "You mean to tell me that Daniel prayed one of the longest recorded prayers in the Bible just to ask for forgiveness and another opportunity?" Precisely. His objectives were to say what *needed* to be said, no matter how long it took, and to say it *from the heart*.

These are crucial principles not only for recovery prayer but also for any interpersonal communication related to recovery needs. If we are to get beyond the past and effectively grow through giving and receiving forgiveness and "another chance," we must invest the time to express (and hear) whatever needs to be said, and it must come from the depths of our hearts. Short of that kind of in-depth communication, we haven't done more than engage in surface chit-chat.

ANSWERED PRAYERS: THE TIMING FACTOR

It is striking that Daniel was still "speaking and praying" when his answer to prayer arrived (9:20). "At the beginning" of Daniel's time of mourning and prayer, "the word went out" from God to dispatch His answer without delay (9:23).[11]

Talk about fast service! Wouldn't it be great if all our prayers were answered this quickly? Not necessarily. Sure, some needs are split-second—meaning that if it doesn't come at that very moment, it's all over. And sometimes the Lord apparently chooses to encourage His children by a rapid answer to prayer. But not all Daniel's prayers were answered lickety-split.

A considerably different sense of prayer response time emerges in the very next chapter of Daniel. In 10:2-3 we read of the aged prophet mourning and fasting "for three entire weeks." Apparently Daniel is just as earnest as he was in 9:3, since he was fasting in both instances. So why the time lag in Daniel 10?

The answer emerging in 10:12-14 is related to spiritual warfare. The answer to Daniel's prayers was somehow hindered by demonic forces in the unseen realm, causing the delay.[12] All the while, though, Daniel was learning afresh the principle of perseverance in prayer.

Answers to recovery prayers can go either way. God undoubtedly esteems the person who is courageous enough to pursue recovery (9:23), and his or her prayers may be answered instantaneously. Of course, other factors, including spiritual warfare, can delay such answers.[13]

Whatever the reasons for delayed answers to prayer, the person in recovery must learn to continue in the process of prayer. Since the overall time frame of recovery is normally a lengthy process, we should not expect that the Lord would cut across the grain of what He is teaching us about persevering and being consistent in other areas to produce instant answers to prayer. That way, when an immediate answer from the Lord does appear, we will be doubly grateful, instead of resentful when it doesn't happen that way.

ANGELS WATCHING OVER ME

Even as demonic forces are at work, attempting to stop at least some answers to believers' prayers (Daniel 10:13), so God's angels are involved in the process of "escorting" answers from the Lord to His people (9:21-23). This should not surprise us, considering that the writer of Hebrews says of angels: "Are they not all ministering spirits, sent out to render service for the sake of those who will inherit salvation?" (1:14).

Many times believers with recovery needs feel generally unworthy and unimportant, and that feeling carries over to their prayer life. This passage in Daniel 9, coupled with Hebrews 1:14, can help clear up that misunderstanding on the levels of both head and heart.

Hebrews 1:14 seems to make it clear that the Lord has a sort of dispatch service for helping Christians. It appears that God sends out guard details, possibly "strength-enhancers" (see 2 Corinthians 12:9-10), and absolutely no telling what else, in order to deal with certain needs and dangers.

What a mind-picture that is! If you remember seeing John Hinckley's attempt to assassinate President Ronald Reagan, you might also recall all those Secret Service agents coming out of the woodwork. God's unseen angelic agents are protecting Christians, who are very special in the eyes of the Commander-in-Chief of the universe. After all, why would the Lord go to all the trouble of protecting each believer, including those hurting desperately with longstanding recovery issues, if we weren't very important to Him and "highly esteemed" in His fatherly eyes?

GREAT EXHAUSTION, GREAT ESTEEM

Recovery issues are emotionally and physically exhausting to face. Daniel's recovery proved to be no exception to that rule. His answer to prayer came at a point of "extreme weariness" (9:21). Though that might be due merely to the effects on an old man of a long period of prayer, there seems good reason to think more is involved.[14]

In the face of the traumatic visions in Daniel 8 and 11–12, he became physically exhausted and ill (8:27, 10:8). In Daniel 9, God's decision to give Judah "another chance" was a joyful thing in the godly prophet's life. Also, Daniel had just poured out his heart before the Lord in his grand "Prayer for Recovery." In his transparency before God, he had faced and confessed profound internal pain and shame. Who wouldn't feel like a wrung-out dishrag, emotionally and physically, in such circumstances?

But tired as he was, Daniel could be at peace for having carried through his great recovery prayer. He also could rest assured that he was highly esteemed in the eyes of the Lord. Those two factors undoubtedly provided great comfort in his heart for the rest of his life.

Some people may take for granted peace of heart and a proper sense of esteem.[15] But those qualities are in critically short supply among people needing recovery, including Christians. Daniel's example of recovery prayer can also be a helpful model for many who are overwhelmed with the need for internal peace and proper esteem for other reasons. Recovery prayer may leave you in a state of "extreme weariness," but the realization that you have been granted forgiveness and that you are highly esteemed makes it worth it many times over.

WHO'S WHO AMONG PRAYER-WARRIORS

It is fairly well known that Daniel made it into the "Hall of Fame" of Hebrews 11. The phrase "shut the mouths of lions" in Hebrews 11:33 can hardly apply to anyone else.

But I think the best part of the Hebrews Hall of Fame passage is at the end. As great as all the examples of faith are in that chapter, entrance to the Hall of Fame is still open to any person of proper faith. As the chapter concludes: "apart from us they should not be made perfect" (11:40).

You and I have a good shot at the Hall of Fame. Fantastic! But equally exciting is that we are also on the right path to be recognized in "Who's Who Among Prayer Warriors."

What are the criteria for selection in this Hall of Fame? Let's look at our distinguished first honoree, Daniel. Based on his example, there will be a lot of recovery prayer warriors admitted to this Who's Who. The qualities that mark Daniel as a great man of prayer—earnestness, openness, responsibility, "personal touch," and "hanging in there"—lay the foundation for recovery prayer. If you are working on these qualities in your "vertical recovery" (between you and the Lord), you are living a "Who's Who" prayer style that is "highly esteemed."

WHO'S CALLING THE SHOTS HERE?

The answer to Daniel's prayer is in its own way as remarkable as the amazing prayer itself (9:24-27). The "Seventy Weeks Prophecy," as it is often called, has been the subject of so much interest and controversy that it has often overshadowed the recovery prayer from which it emerged.[16]

That imbalance is unfortunate, because failure to pay close attention to Daniel's prayer leaves us "flying blind" in approaching the prophecy. Many aspects of Daniel 9:24-27 are the fruit of roots deep in the soil of the previous recovery prayer.

To a degree, our discussion in this book will seek to correct that balance. We will be looking at the prophecy in 9:25-27 as it relates significantly to understanding the material in 9:24, which is most directly related to Daniel's recovery prayer and thus most directly applicable to recovery issues today. This material in 9:24 can also be seen as the key to the overall interpretation of the prophecy in the succeeding three verses.[17]

Sometimes we get so caught up in answering the questions related to *when* the "Seventy Weeks" are fulfilled in history that we do a far from adequate job on *why* this specific prophecy was given in the first place. That will be our primary focus in the rest of this chapter.

Another dimension we tend to neglect in our preoccupation with prophetic details is found in the "sandwich" effect created by the repetition of the idea "decreed" in 9:24,27.[18] The significance seems to be that all of this will happen only because the God of recovery graciously answered Daniel's prayer and "decreed" this outcome.

Such an implication points us directly to the sovereignty of God in wider history and also in individual and relational recovery.[19] That sense of God's power and control summed up in "decreed" may seem harsh at first glance. But our individual choices would be without wider meaning and direction if God were not equally the Sovereign Lord of our individual recovery as well as of Judah's national restoration.

As we turn to consider the purpose of the "Seventy Weeks" prophecy in Daniel 9:24, let's stop and check our spiritual lenses. Do we need to adjust them in order to avoid a nearsighted focus on minor details? The view is so much better when we can back away and see clearly the big picture of the Sovereign Lord who calls the shots of history and has graciously decreed "another chance" for His people.

LET'S TRY IT AGAIN

Daniel 9:24 begins by setting up a time framework that would have sounded eerily familiar to Daniel. The reason for this is pictured in table 6.1. In His gracious choice to give exiled Judah "another chance," God looks back at the failed past of His people much as Daniel had done in beginning his prayer.

Table 6.1
Another Chance from God: Why Are There *Seventy* Sevens?

70 x 7 = 490	(70 Years)	70 (x) 7s "decreed" = 490
70 unkept Sabbath years	DANIEL ⇦ IN ⇨ EXILE	
ca. 1,400–600 BC		(?)
(2 Chronicles 36:21)	(Jeremiah 25, 29)	(Daniel 9:24-27)
BLOWN *FIRST* CHANCE	CONSEQUENCES	EQUAL *SECOND* CHANCE

God, of course, had absolutely nothing to be ashamed of or to confess, as Daniel did on behalf of sinful Judah. But He takes their lengthy "first chance" into account from another angle. While He most certainly has forgiven their sin, as Daniel had just requested, the Lord had not "forgotten" in the way that too many of us understand that concept.[20] Instead, He wants His people to remember that first period in the Promised Land every time they hear the "Seventy Weeks" prophecy.

Why? Is the Lord being spiteful or cruel, rubbing Judah's nose in her sin? No. He wants her to learn from her mistakes so she will not repeat them in the future (the period prophesied in 9:24-27). He is intent that the "second chance" will not turn out like the first (the Babylonian Exile).

Let's think about that "blown first chance," as Daniel would have done upon first hearing 9:24. During the roughly eight centuries that the Jews had been in their own land between the Exodus period and the exile to Babylon, they had been inconsistent in keeping the sabbatical year regulations in the Law of Moses. Second Chronicles 36:21 specifies that the seventy-year exile from the land made up for seventy sabbatical years unkept over the centuries. This means that well over half the time (490 of about 800 years), the Jews did not comply with God's requirements, thus storing up the just consequences that befell Judah in the Exile.

From a recovery standpoint, this is a *reality*-based diagnosis on God's part. He does not portray everything done in those 800 years as evil. There were more than three centuries of obedience, probably including a good bit of King Josiah's reign, when Daniel was a boy, just before the Exile.

On the other hand, the Lord doesn't gloss over the sins of the past, even though He has forgiven them. If the Jews are to go back into the same location and context where they committed all that sin before, they must learn and be accountable. This is similar to what alcoholics or other individuals with compulsive patterns must undergo. Staying on the straight and narrow path of recovery usually requires learning from past mistakes, developing new habits, and either staying away from the old haunts or being *incredibly* careful and accountable.

Finally, there is the future outlook. Plotting out the exact number of years that had been "blown" in sin the first time around indicates that God was taking His people back for another run-through so they could get it right this time.

An analogy to this second run-through is the production of taped television shows and movies. If the cast doesn't get it right the first time, they do another take until the director is satisfied that it is right. Of course, in television and the movies, there may be numerous takes. With Judah, God is graciously granting only a "double-take."

GOD'S "SECOND-CHANCE" AGENDA

When the angel Gabriel tells Daniel that his people and the holy city will get a "new lease on life," he also shares God's stated agenda to be accomplished during the period of the "Seventy Weeks" (490 years).[21] There are six items God has put Himself on the line to fulfill (9:24). The question from our vantage point is, "Have these things all occurred in history, or not?"

Some hold that all six have been fulfilled in the first Advent of Jesus Christ.[22] Others believe that something less than total fulfillment has taken place so far.[23] The difference it makes is whether the Jews' "second chance" was completed when Christ was on earth (or shortly thereafter), or whether a part remains to be finished at His Second Coming.

Let's consider the "agenda items" briefly in regard to implications for recovery needs. The first three all deal with sinfulness: "transgression," "sin," and "iniquity." These, of course, were the kinds of behavior that brought on the Babylonian Exile (9:5,11).

In ways not stated clearly in this passage, sin in its various forms will be finally and decisively done away with. But at this stage, the only one of the three that has certainly been fulfilled is the third item: Christ's "atonement for iniquity." Both believers, generally, and those with recovery needs, specifically, can be truly grateful that our sins are paid for in full, and that the Lord is deeply involved in putting a decisive end to the sinfulness that prompts and reproduces abuse and dysfunctional behavior generation after generation.

The final three items on the Lord's list are much harder to categorize. All clearly deal with positive factors, the basic opposites of sin. It is possible that "everlasting righteousness" has basically the same force as "everlasting life" (John 3:16). If so, that element of Daniel 9:24 may have been fulfilled in Christ's work on the cross. However, vision and prophecy clearly was not "sealed" even at the end of the last book of the Bible (Revelation 22:10). Also, it is much more likely that "the most holy" refers to the Holy of Holies in the Jewish Temple, as it is used elsewhere in the Old Testament, rather than to Christ. Since the Temple was heavy on Daniel's heart in his recovery prayer, that almost clinches the identification.

Whatever these final three elements mean in detail, they clearly envision a situation in which: (1) righteousness will not be just the exclusive property of the Lord and the godly few; (2) God will not need to send visions and prophets to His hard-hearted, denying people; (3) holiness will be recognized and cherished.

Coupled with the banishment of sin described in the first three items, here we see a description of a "fully recovered" society. Only when all six of these factors have taken full effect with humankind will the restoration from the age-long warping effects of sin be utterly eliminated. But we can look ahead with this realistic hope only because the gracious Lord of recovery saw fit to give His people another chance in answer to Daniel's majestic prayer for recovery.

PART
2

A Process of
Of
Recovery

7
SURVIVING A CRISIS AT MID-LIFE

I do not like the concept of "mid-life crisis." In fact, I despise the idea! But it's not so much what it *means* that bothers me. It's the *implied behavior* that irritates me.

Maybe you haven't ever thought about the gap between the actual meaning of "mid-life crisis" and the popular picture it conjures up for the average person. But that's the reason why I refuse to use that terminology unless I am absolutely forced to.

Strictly speaking, the concept is helpful in focusing attention on the confusing issues that must be faced in transition through a difficult stage of life. But in its popular distortion, it usually invites most people to assume the worst—which characteristically includes having an affair and doing a lot of childish, stupid things that tend to shatter families and wreck reputations (if not whole careers).

How did this invalid shift of focus from *difficult issues* to *disgusting behavior* take place?

GETTING BEYOND THE "MIDDLE-AGED CRAZIES"

I first remember the M-word emerging in popular American vocabulary during the mid-to-late seventies. I distinctly recall some people using the phrase "middle-aged crazies" almost interchangeably with the one I'm boycotting.

No wonder this misused idea took on the tone of a sleazy soap-opera lifestyle! If we expect almost everyone to act crazy during a certain difficult stage of life, then a lot of otherwise intelligent people will make good on those expectations. They will assume they have societal "permission" to suspend their responsible behavior temporarily because they have fallen prey to a serious case of the "middle-aged crazies."

Please don't misunderstand me. I certainly am not making light of the tremendously confusing, even highly painful, issues encountered in the broader mid-life developmental period (somewhere between the early thirties to the mid-fifties or thereabouts). I am, however, taking dead aim on the false equation that essentially asserts: Confusing Internal Struggles + Permissive Societal Expectations = "Wild and Crazy Behavior."

That equation simply does not compute . . . except as a lame excuse. After all, we expect Christian teenagers, living through the *other* most confusing and stressful period in life, to make responsible moral decisions to stand up to brutal peer pressure regarding drugs, alcohol, and sexual activity. Why would we expect any less of believers who have progressed to their mid-life years? It's a mystery to me.

FACING A CRISIS AT MID-LIFE RESPONSIBLY

I hereby propose that evangelicals cease and desist from employing the M-word. In its place, I suggest we substitute the slightly bulkier "crisis at mid-life." Why? It retains the positive objective content of its contaminated twin without the lopsided negative cultural baggage.

People all around us *are* facing crises of severe emotional and relational proportions during mid-life. To say otherwise is to proclaim that the world is flat whenever we pull our head up out of the sand. And if we are at all honest, we will readily admit that the numbers increasingly include true believers in Jesus Christ.

However, admitting that there is reason to go on crisis alert is not the same as rolling over and playing dead regarding the outcome and effects of that crisis. If anything, crisis alert is the best mode for heading off at the pass (or at least holding to a minimum) destructive effects and outcomes.

Alternatively (and not much of a choice, I might add), two common responses inevitably result in clean-up detail for the wreckage of lives and reputations on the other end of the crisis once the dust finally settles. The first response denies there is a problem by refusing to face up to escalating internal stresses and issues that are cracking the surface and creating a crisis atmosphere. The second response admits there is a crisis but does nothing about it by passively "going with the flow."

The first (lack of) response sets you up to be blind-sided by the more intense aspects of the crisis. Before you have a chance to come to terms with your struggles honestly, you're dazed and likely down for the count. This angle forces you into playing a bewildered game of emotional and relational catch-up—to say the very least.

The second "response" is only preferable if you are the kind of person who wants to know ahead of time that you are going to be in a destructive and painful car wreck. The catch is that you must passively refuse to take any substantial steps to prevent it. You simply get on the emotional and relational roller-coaster and wait to hear the first crunch of metal.

From my own experience with recovery issues, over fifteen years of pastoral counseling, and close association with other pastors and counselors, it's clear to me that there is only one choice, although initially it may not seem to be such a happy one. The remaining option is to admit there is a crisis and face up to it as soon as the warning signs begin to show. In that way, accountability, support, and encouragement measures can be put into action in order to minimize storm damage at the end of the painful duration.

AN APOSTLE'S CRISIS AT MID-LIFE

If you are surfacing or wrestling with such issues in your own life, you may find it comforting to realize that no less a spiritual giant than the Apostle Paul plowed this rocky field before. Among the most important principles that he learned is: *Growing spiritually through a crisis at mid-life requires admitting your weakness and relying on God's grace.*

This chapter will trace the general contours of Paul's middle-years crisis, especially in regard to the kinds of *external* problems and difficulties he was facing during that period of his life. That kind of autobiographical information about Paul's life is most readily available in 2 Corinthians 11:18–12:10. Table 7.1 (page 102) tracks the insightful parallels between that painfully personal section and the *internal-emotional* perspective offered by Philippians 3:2-16, the passage that is the expositional basis of chapters 8–12 in this book.

Table 7.1
Paul's Recovery: A Prolonged Crisis at Mid-Life

	Immediate Context			
Mid-to-Later Fifties (2 Corinthians)	Aggressive Jewish False "Apostles" (Chs. 10–13)	Basis for "Boasting": General Jewish Background (11:22)	Cataloging Service and Suffering: What Happened on the Surface (11:23–12:8)	God's Grace Operative in Human Suffering/Weakness (12:9–10)
Age in Writing	Immediate Context	Remembering Pre-Christian Life (until mid-thirties)	Happenings Since Conversion to Christ (mid-thirties–mid-fifties, for the most part)	The "Bottom Line": Wise Perspective for Recovery
(Philippians) Early Sixties	(3:2-16) Aggressive Jewish False Teachers	(3:4-6) Reasons for "Confidence in the Flesh": More Detailed Jewish Background	(3:7-11) Analyzing/Explaining Recovery: What Happened Spiritually/Emotionally	(3:12-16) Human Responsibility to Choose and Mature Beyond Past Dysfunction/Understanding

Some biblical commentators have puzzled over the relationship between these passages, which are two of the three longest self-revealing portions in all of Paul's letters.[1] Since both were written in response to the problem of false teachers who place great confidence in natural human strength, they clearly emerge out of almost identical concerns.[2] As table 7.1 details, they face these challenges in amazingly "hand-in-hand" ways. We will mine both passages to discover principles and strategies for *responsibly* facing pressing external problems while simultaneously dealing with internal emotional and spiritual issues.

HOW HIGH IS YOUR PAIN TOLERANCE?

I am not an expert on physical pain. In my lifetime, I've endured a few sprains, a pinched nerve, and a broken bone from athletics. Besides those injuries, a bout with the mumps as a young adult and the viral pneumonia I referred to in chapter 1 are the outer limits of my pain.

On the other hand, my wife lives daily with considerable physical pain because of a bad back. I've spent many hours massaging Cathy's back just so that she could relax enough to get a little sleep. I think of the great discomfort and pain Cathy went through in the pregnancies and births of our three wonderful children. Wow! My physical suffering is most definitely of the "hangnail" variety even compared to those who are close to me.

The Apostle Paul was neither a complainer nor a hypochondriac, but you might wonder the first time you read through the list in 2 Corinthians 11:23-27. Remember also that this was not a full lifetime of suffering, though it would be more than enough. This had all happened to Paul since he had become a servant of Christ, probably around twenty years before he wrote the second letter to the Corinthians.[3]

In an interesting and perhaps significant parallel to the CML issue discussed earlier, Paul appears to have been between thirty and thirty-five years old when he became a Christian. At least part of the confusing onslaught of what I'm calling his "apostolic crisis at mid-life" began shortly thereafter.[4]

Again, it is intriguing that 2 Corinthians was written when Paul would have been just past fifty-five years old, around the age when middle-years issues usually end. Certainly many of the family and societal factors that produce the kind of crises at mid-life (CML) commonly seen today would not have been around in the first century AD. Yet other equally important aspects related to human nature and sin remain virtually unchanged across the centuries and cultures.

At the very least, a plausible age-chronology angle exists for asserting that the various trials that tested Paul's faith, as cataloged in 2 Corinthians 11, happened within the general CML time boundaries.[5] Even if it's a stretch to assert that Paul went through a CML, it is clear that he would have understood and identified with the intense pain, much of it emotional, that many believers are facing at mid-life today.

THE TELLING QUESTION OF COMMITMENT

When people are going through a CML, one crucial area in which many waver is commitment. All too often, whatever long-term commitments are in force when the painful issues begin to surface go up for grabs. This is tragically common even among believers.

The rationalization for this phase in which many individuals bail out of every responsibility they possibly can is that they have been smothered by such obligations and people. Supposedly, they are merely reacting (usually overreacting) to the crushing load of overcommitment and others' control.

Fairly obviously, the two areas in which this common retreat from commitment during a CML is most devastating to believers in Jesus Christ are the human family and the family of God. The relationships that are under the most tension during a CML are usually the two most truly sacred relationships in life: with a life-mate and with our eternal Lord and Savior.

There is a clear similarity between these two primary commitments—horizontal (human-human) and vertical (divine-human). In both cases the decisive moment of trust produces a public form of covenanted (contracted) relationship. Also, both require that the relationship with a life-partner be worked out daily on the basis of trust.

Some might shortsightedly conclude that the Apostle Paul had less to deal with in the relational commitment area because there is no indication that he was married. Technically, it is correct that Paul did not have a "wife." However, the passage before us gives strong indication that Paul was, in a manner of speaking, "married." Not only that, this marital relationship of sorts had to be safeguarded and developed through Paul's prolonged CML. Finally (and this is a very important applicational point), all of this was happening alongside the ongoing testing and stretching of his commitment as a servant of Christ.

Paul was, in effect, "married" to the church through his apostolic ministry. He certainly exhibited the kind of "intense concern," bordering on worry, for the object of his commitment that befits an earnest husband. There is even a certain amount of normal "jealousy" on Paul's part.[6]

What can we learn from Paul's CML on this crucial issue of primary commitments? First, he does not view his relationships with Christ and the church as additional problems in the midst of all the pain he went through over an extended period.[7] If anything, they were why he stayed with it through all the confusion and suffering (which may not have been entirely sorted out in this way until Paul sat down and "journaled" 2 Corinthians 11:23–12:10 under divine inspiration). They provided anchors in the midst of the storms (and largely uncharted emotional waters) the apostle had to weather.

Second, and especially hard to grasp for men who were schooled in the John Wayne brand of masculinity, it is entirely possible to admit your weakness and end up stronger in your primary relationships as a result. Paul knew full well that his transparency might appear foolish to spiritually immature Corinthian readers. But owning up to weakness (in Paul's case, whether in regard to personal recovery issues, to his commitment to the Lord, or to his commitment to the Church) is the channel through which God's healing and sustaining power flows.[8]

BLESSINGS OUT OF HEALED BRUISES

As I have learned more about recovery these past couple of years, I have come to realize how fortunate I am that I was not physically abused. I did sustain a lot of bruises and the like while playing sports. But my physical bruises occurred within appropriate boundaries of games I loved, not in "out of bounds" terrorizing by one who is supposed to be loving.

Paul took more than his share of bruises during his CML period. In the passage before us in 2 Corinthians, you don't have to read any further than the initial references to imprisonments, innumerable beatings, and severe whippings to start wincing with pain. This guy really went through the mill! If we didn't have such plentiful additional evidence that Paul was a balanced mature believer, we might think that he was a glutton for punishment, maybe even a borderline masochist. When Paul had the blues, it probably had almost as much to do with the color of his skin as it did with his emotions.

Like a victim of physical abuse, Paul should not have had to go through such ordeals at the hands of the "Jews," the "Gentiles," and especially the "false brethren" in the churches. Unlike many abuse victims, though, Paul never implies that he somehow "asked for" or deserved that painful and unjust treatment. He simply acknowledges realistically what he had to go through in connection with the life-changing lesson that he sorted out from being a "battered person."

That lesson is also related to admitting your weakness, as we saw earlier in this chapter. It involves a major reorientation to those painful events that have scarred your life and relationships. But it's worth the effort because it allows you to take with you for the rest of your earthly pilgrimage a glass that is half full (and filling up) of God's grace instead of one that is half empty, retaining a painful and bitter aftertaste.

In order to appreciate that incredible lesson, we'll be doing some in-depth spadework in this extended passage (2 Corinthians 11:22–12:10) on the interaction between, on the one hand, human suffering and weakness and, on the other hand, divine power and grace. We will see that they have a unique "hand in glove" relationship.

THE THORNBUSH NEXT TO THE POWER PLANT

I must still be growing because I am still learning new and valuable things all the time. One recent insight I've come across is that there is more good about a thorn than knowing that you can often locate a rose nearby.

The "thorns" that pierce believers' lives with so much distracting frustration and pain always grow next to a power plant. Whenever various thorny situations remind you afresh of your weakness, don't be ashamed or despairing. Be open to the reality of those weak areas and plug in to God's power plant (12:9-10).

At the points where you are so emotionally overburdened or depleted that you think your spiritual battery is almost dead, the Lord is ready to give you much more than a spiritual-emotional jumpstart. He is lovingly serious about serving as a long-term "alternative power source" for you to use in furthering your personal recovery, relationships, and responsibilities.

Paul certainly took his spiritual-emotional extension cord to the "power plant" while his "thorn in the flesh" was still very painful. Since the amazing event narrated in 12:2-4 had happened about fourteen years before the writing of 2 Corinthians, Paul had had a thorny time of it from around age forty on.[9]

There is nothing to be gained from trying to determine the exact nature of Paul's thorn in the flesh. There are as many theories as there are candidates in early presidential primaries. Besides, the better part of wisdom is to realize that if the Lord had wanted anyone beyond the original readers to know what it was, he would have told us (or at least left more clues).

If Paul *had* nailed down exactly what his "thorn in the flesh" consisted of, we would probably limit our application only to very similar situations. So, instead of lamenting his vagueness, we should thank him for implying that there are wider applicational possibilities here for readers in any of a number of thorny situations.

THE UNEASY RELATIONSHIP
BETWEEN THORNS AND BALLOONS

My kids think it's great fun to borrow my razor and shaving cream and attempt to "shave" a balloon. My usual reaction is to find some area where a miniature Mount St. Helens can do only minimal damage. Oh, yes—and we also need to know who is going to clean up the mess.

Paul must have felt like he was a balloon being shaved by his "thorn." Look at what was at stake: His reputation and ministry could easily have been hindered or even shattered. But there was also the increasingly obvious realization that God wanted to keep Paul humble and Satan wanted him humiliated.

These are big stakes to be playing for during a period of life as unstable and confusing as a CML . . . or anytime, for that matter. But Paul, realizing what was on the line, cooperated in letting the Lord deflate his balloon to a healthy level so that the Devil would not be successful in using the thorn to disastrously burst the apostle's bubble.

Paul might have had something approaching a reason to exalt himself because of the heavenly understanding he derived. But the rest of us are usually in danger of plain old self-deceived self-glorification. And in the process, Satan takes all the wind out of us in what can be an explosive downfall.

Paul's apostolic warning to the wise is that God's cure for being suffering and weak (the status of most people entering recovery) is definitely *not* to be successful and strong (the pedestal from which you need a parachute to fall without becoming a grease spot)! That's not to say that He won't use someone in a successful and strong way, as He did Paul. But He prefers to use those who are honest about their lives in acknowledging their human frailty.

WHEN GOD SEEMS LIKE EBENEZER SCROOGE

I think our consumer-oriented culture has had a bigger impact than we might like to admit on the quality and quantity of our prayer. Many of us have bought an understanding of prayer as some kind of 800 number to God for the purpose of ordering whatever we want, free of charge.

With this prevailing mentality, it's no wonder that some pragmatic people tend to give up on prayer when they don't see immediate dividends from their time investment.

But think about it. Did God love Paul any less than Daniel because He delayed, then said no to Paul, although He had given Daniel an immediate, positive answer?[10] In what sense is a God who would never turn down a prayer request any more "loving" than a God who sometimes says no in the best interests of the one making the request? Which is a truer picture of God—a permissive "sugar daddy" who spoils his children, or a truly caring and loving Father?

Prayer often gets short shrift with those having recovery issues, but for very different reasons. Coming from backgrounds in which they have encountered either dictatorial, distant, absentee, untrustworthy, or abusive fathers, these individuals' conception of "father" tells them that the heavenly Father won't listen, care, or be there for them any more than their human variety was. That false impression is often furthered by "no" or "wait" answers.

Paul's emphasis on prayer elsewhere in his letters indicates that he would not have given up easily or prayed self-serving prayers.[11] However, when you're dialing 911 in the middle of a crisis situation, you don't want to be put on hold or told to find help elsewhere. So, I'm sure Paul was hardly elated when he cried out in pain repeatedly to the Lord and the answer kept coming back, "I'm not going to take the thorn away, Paul. It will teach you invaluable lessons about My power and grace."[12] But God did answer Paul by telling him that the thorn was tolerable because he could spell spiritual "relief" in the midst of painful circumstances G-R-A-C-E.

SUFFICIENT GRACE: WHAT IT IS AND ISN'T

Among the greatest needs of people with recovery issues is to understand God's grace. Out of such dysfunctional family and relational backgrounds, it is entirely possible to give an orthodox theological answer about divine grace while not having a clue at the "gut level" to what it means in practice.

But at the least, an accurate theological definition is a place to start (although too many people also make it their place to end). That may well have been the way it was with the Apostle Paul. As we will see in the next chapter, he grew up in a rigid, basically grace-less environment as a member of the Pharisees, the strictest sect of Judaism.

But Paul didn't remain caught in that smothering web of legalism. He determined that he would "grow in grace," as the Apostle Peter later urged all Christians to do (2 Peter 3:18). This growth became so consistent and pronounced that Paul's usage of the term *grace* in his epistles is the most substantial and detailed in the entire New Testament.[13]

"Undeserved favor" is the most commonly used compact definition of grace. We will work from that perspective in seeking to understand just exactly how God's grace is "sufficient" for the person beset by weakness and difficulties. That can be done effectively by both contrast and comparison.

Initially, it must be clearly understood that the grace referred to in 2 Corinthians 12:9 is certainly not immediate deliverance from suffering or problems, even though God's power is strongly at work. Second, divine grace does not remove the weaknesses in a person's life. And third, the powerful grace of God does not shy away from taking up residence ("may dwell") in the ongoing weak points in a believer's personality.

These negations are all against the grain of certain imbalanced approaches to "instant healing." Some Bible teachers and groups believe that the Lord heals emotional hurts and struggles all at once, as we fully turn them over to Him by the prayer of faith. Others teach that the healing takes place at the point of initial salvation through total commitment to Christ's lordship.

Both of these angles would have been news to Paul! In spite of his believing prayer, he was not instantly healed from his recovery-oriented issues, which will be handled in some depth in the remaining chapters. Yet God had still promised that His sufficient grace would be there for Paul. What did that mean?

Among its most important features in this context, it means that the Lord's grace is "enough" to deal with the problems of each day, from the hangnails to the heaviest. It is not far from the mark to see God's grace as the emotional "daily bread" for the believer struggling with deep and difficult issues.

Second, God's undeserved favor can grow and become more powerful in our lives even though the weaknesses still exist. Thus we should neither cover up our weaknesses out of shame nor expect God's power to overwhelm them anytime soon. The present tenses "is sufficient" and "is perfected" in 2 Corinthians 12:9 indicate a process at work, which to one extent or another is a recovery process.

Finally, human strength is closer to self-delusion than to God's grace. A strong, self-sufficient person will almost always try to muscle through the difficult situation in his or her own strength. But those who admit their recovery needs can draw upon the Lord's strength and grace from within, no matter how tough things get. *The bottom line is that if you are self-sufficient, you cannot also be grace-sufficient.* Self-sufficient will prove *in*sufficient when the physical, emotional, or spiritual tough times hit.

PLAYING FROM YOUR WEAKNESSES

Most of us have been raised on the commonsense philosophy of "accenting the positive and eliminating the negative." It not only sounds good, but it usually works well in maximizing the factors in our favor. Playing from personal strengths is the foundational game plan of countless strong and immensely talented champions.

That is not the Lord's game plan for our entire lives, however. He wants us to play from our weaknesses, also. There is a good reason for this seemingly ironic outlook: facing *our* weaknesses plays to *His* strength. In that way, says Paul, "when I am weak, then I am strong" (12:10) by the Lord's gracious, always sufficient power.

This understanding made it possible for the apostle to cope with and grow through the list of difficult and abusive factors listed in 2 Corinthians 12:10—troubles that were still continuing in his life. It also lends great hope to us today. We can take heart in knowing that even if our painful background weaknesses and problems remain through our recovery process, God's grace and power can still be operative in and through our lives.

In the next chapter, our focus will shift to Philippians 3 and Paul's complementary description of the recovery process, including implications concerning his own CML. Before leaving the great apostle's letters to the church at Corinth, though, we do well to recall his plea for proper godly perspective in 1 Corinthians 1:27: "God has chosen the weak things of the world to shame the things which are strong."

If your background has helped you become emotionally strong and healthy, be thankful to the Lord for that blessing! But if that strength has prompted you to deny that others have deep recovery hurts or related weaknesses, the Lord and Paul have a message: *Think again! You have been blinded by your strength to its great rarity in the church (1:26), assuming that everyone should be just like you. That is a dangerously boastful outlook (1:29). So humbly seek the Lord, who gives grace and power to the weak and hurting and proclaims human strength to be a strong self-delusion.*

CHAPTER
8

GETTING BEYOND
THE GOOD FRONT

Natural illumination can cause you to see things in a whole different light. That was especially obvious to me when I attended a unique out-door theater production back in 1974 in Palo Duro Canyon, outside of Amarillo, Texas.

In far West Texas, at the edge of the central time zone, it does not get dark in mid-summer until after 9:30 p.m. Since this performance of the musical *Texas* began at 8:00, well over half the show took place in daylight instead of under the designed stage lighting.

When *Texas* began, the actors looked very strange indeed. Their makeup appeared to be twice as thick as necessary. In fact, the effect was more like a group of puppets than human actors. I honestly wondered if there was some unstated reason for their almost bizarre appearance.

Darkness gradually enclosed the open-air theater. As twilight faded into night, a drastic change in appearance slowly took place before my eyes. The transformation in the way the actors on stage looked was so substantial that I completely forgot the actual play itself. To this day, I could not tell you anything about the production, although I will never forget the makeup on those actors.

That eerie night at the musical drove home to me the reality of an important principle: *How you are in the light of reality may be quite different from your made-up stage presence.*

BIBLICAL LIGHT ON THE SUBJECT

The Apostle Paul develops this principle in some depth in Philippians 3:2-6. He understood it well because he had worn heavy "personality makeup" all of his earlier life. It was only when the supernatural "Light of the world," the resurrected Christ, met Paul on the Damascus Road that he began to see his life in a true light.

As a result of Paul's new insight into himself, his former "candy-coated" approach had become disgusting to him. When he realized that the same kind of front was being used to impress the Philippian Christians, he knew he had to shed some realistic light on the subject.

For the purpose of enlightening and protecting his readers, Paul drew a severe contrast between those who wear spiritual and emotional masks and the people of the Light. To reinforce his point, the apostle dug up his own dusty old mask, hoping that his hearers would not make the same mistake that he had.

I really appreciate what Paul was seeking to accomplish in Philippians 3:2-6. That's because I had put on my own mask at one time, though it was certainly not as impressive as Paul's. In my case, as a "floating personality" who had little idea of who I was on the inside, I decided somewhere along the way to present as "accomplished" an external image of myself as possible. Besides creating a positive impact on others, I was hoping I might even convince *myself* that some of these external factors made me an acceptable, perhaps even a significant, person.

There is, however, a major difference between Paul's experience and my own. There is good reason to think that Paul began dealing with what I would call his recovery issues soon after his conversion. By contrast, I managed to make it through twenty years as a Christian before I became aware those issues even existed.

Why did it take me so long to wake up? The only reasons I can offer at this point are: (1) I was a real ace at denial and avoidance of painful issues; (2) my wake-up call didn't ring until I was flattened by viral pneumonia in 1990, while Paul's was a front-end load on the road to Damascus.

It doesn't really matter, however, whether recovery-related needs surface at conversion or many years later. They have basically the same force whether we became a Christian as a small child or in our adult years. If our awakening occurs later in life we may wish we had begun earlier, but reality forces us to make the best of where we are in life when the truth dawns on us.

You may need to mourn what you missed (or had to go through). But you can't go back and start over again. Instead, you must untangle yourself from the hurtful impact of the past and go on with your new biblically informed "life in the light."[1]

WHO ARE THESE "DOGS," ANYWAY?

Enough about Paul and myself for now. While both of us came to understand the personality "makeup" we had worn, the Philippians were being wooed by a group of mobile teachers who apparently had not come to terms with the fronts they were putting up.

We don't know much about these teachers. Fortunately, however, we can piece together enough from this passage to put us on red alert when we see similar situations today.[2]

What kind of image did these false teachers project? What were they really like in the supernatural light that Paul shined on their lives? Were they just putting their best foot forward, or was something much more dangerous going on?

The answer to the first of these questions is probably the opposite of the way Paul describes them to his readers in Philippi. Paul is pointedly telling it like it is, not for a millisecond playing the diplomat in the face of these "visiting professors." Thus it is safe to say that the invaders presented themselves as believers in Christ, but also the cream of Jewish law-keepers, especially emphasizing the rite and sign of covenant circumcision.

A very natural question at this point is, "How could the largely Gentile church, with only a sprinkling of Jewish influence, get sucked in by this Jewish legalism?" Paul knew the answer from his last visit to the church in Jerusalem. After Paul told James and the elders of the church about his ministry, they shared with him what they were up against:

You see, brother, how many thousands there are among the
Jews of those who have believed, and they are all zealous for
the Law; and they have been told about you, that you are teach-

ing all the Jews who are among the Gentiles to forsake Moses,
telling them not to circumcise their children nor to walk according
to the customs. (Acts 21:20-21)

Since a great proportion of the Jerusalem church was in violent
disagreement with Paul no more than four or five years earlier than his
letter to the Philippians, it is not unlikely that some among them formed
a "vigilante band" of sorts to go forth and correct the errors that Paul
had been promoting.[3] Since there was no synagogue in Philippi,[4] these
zealots would have focused on the church in the city to accomplish its
mission.

This was no laughing matter! As Paul had warned the Galatian
Christians some years before:[5]

Behold I, Paul, say to you that if you receive circumcision,
Christ will be of no benefit to you. And I testify again to every
man who receives circumcision, that he is under obligation to
keep the whole Law. (Galatians 5:2-3)

Suffice it to say that buying into this kind of Jewish legalism is
essentially to depart from Christ (Galatians 5:4), no matter what kind
of lip-service to Christianity such legalists might give. Thus, in Paul's
view, whenever even much more subtle forms of legalism begin to make
inroads among God's people, the reality of true Christianity is being
escorted to the door by those who think outward works can make them
more spiritually impressive.

That is exactly why Paul's description in Philippians 3:2 is so caus-
tic. He sees right through the facade of their denial and turns the tables
on these self-deluded Jewish teachers. Most likely these aggressive Jews
had looked down their noses at the Gentile believers in Philippi, calling
them unflattering names such as "dogs," "evil workers," and of course,
"uncircumcised pagans." The apostle counters that, from the standpoint
of spiritual reality, it is the legalists who deserve to be called these things
and worse.

Frankly, I seriously doubt that any of the Jewish legalists "saw
the light" as a result of Paul's argument in this passage. That would
have been wonderful, but legalism is an extremely tough nut to crack,
especially in tandem with its blind cousin denial.[6] Because legalists

are incredibly farsighted (they can see everyone else's problems but not their own), when they team up with deniers on the subject of internal spiritual and emotional reality it becomes a "blind leading the blind" situation.

TRUE WORSHIP AND BIBLICAL RECOVERY

Paul did not launch his severe criticism without offering a healthy alternative, however. In essence, Philippians 3:3 indicates that the *outward claims* of the Jewish legalists are actually the *inward reality* for balanced Christians.

In calling believers the "circumcision," Paul is not caving in to the legalists.[7] Rather, he is referring to the inward circumcision of the heart by the Holy Spirit, which he also speaks of in Romans 2:28-29. His strong implication is that external obedience simply does not accomplish what God wants it to unless it has penetrated to the depths of our being and made a real difference.

When Paul continues by describing the circumcised as those "who worship in the Spirit of God" (Philippians 3:3), he almost surely is calling to mind the clear-cut prescription of Christ Himself: "God is spirit, and those who worship Him must worship in spirit and truth" (John 4:24).[8] Accordingly, there is no room for those who concentrate their efforts on external acts of worship. It is the convergence of the power of the Holy Spirit and the Word of God applied in-depth that produces true worship.

Paul really turns the knife on the legalists when he states that healthy believers "glory in Christ Jesus and put no confidence in the flesh" (Philippians 3:3). The bottom line of legalism is always self-glorification and pride (be it ever so subtle) over external accomplishments (confidence in the flesh). Proper self-confidence or self-esteem is based in a realistic self-estimate, not in a catalog of accomplishments or an applause meter.

All this boils down to a face-off over the nature of worship. The legalist steps forward and demands to know how, and how much, you worship, in order to render his or her external judgment. The healthy Christian responds, "It's a worshipful life," then walks away wondering why legalists always swim in the shallow end of the worship pool.

HOW "CONFIDENT" IS CONFIDENCE IN THE FLESH?

Legalists tend to be self-assured. Paul begins to spar with this fleshly cockiness in 3:3-4. After he repeats "confidence in the flesh" three times in two verses, it doesn't take a nuclear physicist to figure out that he has put his finger on the basic problem. Paul has cut through all the potential theological smokescreens to what makes legalists tick: reliance on their natural human resources, abilities, and accomplishments.

This deep-seated mentality is exactly the opposite of the lesson that Paul had to learn the hard way in 2 Corinthians 12:9-10. God refuses to get into a shoving match between His power and our fleshly strength. He simply lets the legalists flex their own muscles for all to see—and continues to work in the lives of those who are weak enough to know that they desperately need the transforming touch of divine power.

How confident is "confidence in the flesh"? Supremely *over*confident, I would suggest. Once our inflated estimate of self gets popped, we finally notice that the pins of humility and reality were there all along.

MY FLESH CAN WHIP YOURS ANY DAY!

Sometimes when people are particularly pompous or obnoxious, you just want to do something to stuff that arrogance back down their throats. Paul decides that the situation in Philippi is just such an occasion, and even chooses to beat the Jewish legalists at their own game.

Please note that Paul is not serious for one second about really putting his "confidence in the flesh" (Philippians 3:4). He speaks only hypothetically (he "might" have confidence) and in terms of appearance.[9] He has made that massive mistake in the past, and he will not fall prey to legalism again.

By saying "anyone else" (3:4), Paul is giving notice that he is willing to take on any legalist, anytime, anywhere. It would not be far from the mark to understand Paul's wording as a claim that he could have been the heavyweight champion of legalism if he hadn't dropped out of the sport when he became a Christian. (You can almost see Paul standing in the middle of the ring and exclaiming to the referee, "Bring on the next legalist contender. I'll knock him right on his pompous laurels!")

I'm glad Paul is the one duking it out with all those legalists. I was never more than a second banana legalist, and I couldn't get my external act together enough to take on all comers, as Paul was meticulously qualified to do (3:5-6). Besides, what I'm really interested in doing is giving those knocked-out legalists a big dose of grace (2 Corinthians 12:9) to clear their groggy heads and hearts.

A MODEL RÉSUMÉ

Another image for Paul's confrontation with the legalists could be the battle of the résumés. Paul submits the formal summary of his ultra-impressive pre-Christian life in Philippians 3:5-6. Is there a "Goliath" in the camp of the legalists?

Things get strangely silent on the legalists' side of the aisle when they get a gander at Paul's résumé (refer to table 8.1 for the remaining material in this chapter). Among pretenders to the throne, one résumé after another hits the paper shredder until only Paul's remains.

Table 8.1
Personal Résumé of Saul of Tarsus, Ph.D.

I. PRESENT POSITION
Representative-at-large, Jewish Sanhedrin, Jerusalem, Judea

II. CAREER GOALS
- Full-time persecutor of the church, Damascus, Syria
- Higher-ranking roles among Pharisees or Judaism (as position opens)

III. EDUCATION
Doctor of Pharisaology (highest honors), Gamaliel's Rabbinical College, Jerusalem, Judea

IV. BACKGROUND
- Place of Birth: Tarsus, Cilicia
- Nationality: Jewish
- Tribe of Origin: Benjamin
- Circumcision: On the eighth day (see Mosaic Law)
- Religious Party Affiliation: Pharisees

V. ACCOMPLISHMENTS/HONORS
- *Who's Who Among Hebrews*
- Most Valuable Persecutor, Jewish "Christian" Terminators
- Blameless Lifestyle Certificate, Mosaic Law Inspection Society

For further information, contact Acts 22:3 and Philippians 3:5-6.

Is Paul elated over his resounding victory? Hardly. The championship title is hollow unless the vanquished legalists learn how self-defeating their system truly is and, like Paul, turn from prideful outside-in legalism to the balanced inside-out approach characterizing biblical Christianity and its "comeback twin," biblical recovery.

THE PERFECT HEBREW PEDIGREE

Now that the contest is over, let's do some stop-action analysis of Paul's victorious résumé. Philippians 3:5 gives us the splendid bloodline from which this champion emerged. Paul points to his perfectly timed circumcision right out of the blocks because that's the issue that got the whole competition cranked up back in 3:2. The mention that he came from "the tribe of Benjamin" probably was because Benjamin provided Israel's first king, Saul, for whom the champ was named.[10]

Things start getting really interesting when we run into the phrase "a Hebrew of Hebrews" (3:5). The exact meaning is uncertain, possibly referring to Paul's pure Jewish ancestry or his fluency in the Hebrew language in spite of being raised in Tarsus.[11] Whatever the case, the wording comes off very much like an entry in some prestigious "Who's Who" list in contemporary Judaism.

The last Jewish blueblood factor in Philippians 3:5 is Paul's former status as a Pharisee. That was the strictest party-line lifestyle of that era in Judaism, and Paul went to the top of its class. But, it was also the classic legalistic lifestyle, which Jesus skewered as deceptively beautiful on the outside and dead and hypocritical on the inside (Matthew 23:27).

Do you think Paul might have scored a knockdown on the legalists by recalling his short but brilliant career as a Pharisee? Almost certainly they knew they had taken a big hit from the apostle at that point. If he could turn the Jewish Sanhedrin into a heated brawl by mentioning he was a Pharisee (Acts 23:6-10), why not toss it out at these legalists? They almost certainly sided with the Pharisees straight down the line.

A KILLJOY WITH FOLLOW-THROUGH

Up to this point in Paul's Jewish résumé, you might wonder if he had been merely a mechanical heir to his family's Pharisaic heritage. But the wording "as to zeal, a persecutor of the church" (Philippians 3:6) reveals the pre-Christian legalistic Saul to be a ferocious go-getter, a hard-charging religious fanatic who wouldn't stop until he had angrily stamped out the "heresy" that was Christianity (Acts 9:1-2).

The terribly sad, but very applicable, part of all this was that Paul appeared to have been totally sincere in his misguided zeal. He was also incredibly successful: "advancing in Judaism beyond many of my contemporaries among my countrymen, being more extremely zealous for my ancestral traditions" (Galatians 1:14).

Imagine trying to convince a deeply sincere and tremendously successful person that he desperately needs to face some major-league dysfunction in his life. Good luck!

But Paul could break that one open by telling of his shattering experience of being a sincerely *wrong* and incredibly successful *workaholic who lost everything he had worked for* (Philippians 3:7-8).[12] Being sincere and successful are often merely societally acceptable ways to get away with denial and drivenness, instead of getting honest about recovery.

OUTWARD PERFECTION

Picture yourself in a Marine barracks where the top sergeant is carrying out a white-gloves inspection. If even a speck of dust shows up on those dress gloves, you fail the inspection. Everything has to be perfect to pass.

Retool that picture to focus on religious white gloves carrying out a phenomenally rigorous inspection of the lifestyle of the unsaved Saul of Tarsus. The incredible thing is that not a speck of behavioral dust can be found anywhere. By all appearances, this man is about as close to perfect as humanity can get.

Of course, that wasn't the whole story, just the impressive outer shell. The rest of the story is found in Romans 7:7-11, where Paul admits to a faultline of coveting that had left cracks in the foundation of his life. The appearance of perfection was just a front.

I've had my share of recovery issues to deal with, but perfectionism is not one of them. My office is "organized" around the pile approach. At the end of semesters, the stacks of papers being graded begin to look roughly similar to snow-capped peaks in the Rocky Mountains. I do clean up the mess periodically . . . but then I can't find anything for several weeks until I get my piles back in shape.

Of course, opposites attract, so naturally I married a perfectionist. Bless her heart, Cathy has done well to hang on to her sanity, between very imperfect me and our not-quite-perfect kids (the good news is they are more like Mom than Dad). And she has done a remarkable job, in my estimation, of moderating her compulsive perfectionism.

I think Paul would be as proud of her as I am. For example, Cathy now lets me have a couple of my beloved piles around in clear view when I'm working. She is now more likely to go to bed at night when she is exhausted even though everything is not yet picked up.

If dyed-in-the-wool perfectionists can learn to come to terms with this incredibly frustrating, imperfect world full of imperfect people, there's also realistic hope for the whole range of recovery issues that believers have to face!

LEGALISM PLUS ANGER EQUALS . . .

The apostle gave us a deluxe guided tour of the "makeup" that he wore on tour throughout his earlier life outside Christ. It was a fascinating look behind the scene and the appearances and images that he played out to the hilt.

Paul was truly a study in extremes, almost certainly a complex compulsive personality. On the one hand, he excelled at everything he did. Like Daniel, he was an incredibly high achiever who was always aiming higher. That furious drive for accomplishment and recognition marked his perfectionism and workaholism. Too bad such categories didn't exist back then. Paul would have served as a distinguished prototype in both areas.

Those same markers open windows into a tortured soul. Surely Paul's frustration level was great, given the disparity between his "perfect" projected image (Philippians 3:6) and the "coveting" festering inside him. Also, the incredible commitment and energy he poured into pursuing the church of Jesus Christ left a trail of rage and vindictiveness (Acts 9:1) that went far beyond what might have been expected, especially given the much milder outlook of the unsaved Saul's major professor and mentor, Gamaliel.[13]

What was the personality that had worked its way between the lines of this flawless résumé and out from behind the front that had shielded

Paul's innermost being for so many years? Basically, it was the same subtly proud, legalistic outlook as the Jewish false teachers in Philippi, which is why Paul saw right through them like an X-ray machine.

Two major differences between Paul and the false teachers are worth noting. Both are related to "more so." If the legalists were proud and perfectionistic, Paul was much more so. His intellect, energy, and ambition marked him as a terror among legalists. His example offers great hope for many today in Christian circles who are still enslaved to legalism.

If the legalists were angrily judgmental, Paul was definitely much more so. His rage toward the church was like an unstable bomb liable to explode at any time. Thankfully, the Lord defused that emotional rageaholism through the biblical recovery process (Philippians 3:7-16), transforming Paul into the wise recovery veteran who could write: "Be angry and yet do not sin; do not let the sun go down on your anger, and do not give the devil an opportunity" (Ephesians 4:26-27).

9

GARBAGE IN, GARBAGE OUT

B ecause I was a "floating personality" so much of my life, I didn't have much of a grip on what I was going to do when I grew up. When you don't really know who you are, as I didn't, you tend to consider all kinds of possibilities for future jobs.

Along the way, I thought somewhat seriously about vastly different professions. I actually considered being a pro athlete (dream on!) or coach, a history teacher (relatively close to what I'm doing at this point in my life), and an accountant (my poorly chosen college major). At the time, each of these jobs interested me in some way and seemed plausible.

There were a number of other vocations, however, that I would never have thought of considering in a million years. High on my "no way, no time, no how" list of jobs was trash collector. Sure, I knew that somebody had to deal with all the garbage. But it was not going to be yours truly.

Fortunately for society, not everyone feels the way I did. Sanitation professionals play a very necessary role in society, and definitely an honorable one. We'd be a mess without them.

Also consider how much garbage is "compacted" deep inside the person needing recovery. As that emotional, spiritual, and relational garbage surfaces, it needs to be disposed of properly. But what kind of disposal service handles that kind of garbage?

GOD, THE ULTIMATE GARBAGE DISPOSER

There is just such a garbage business, and it is worldwide in scope. Even though it has no legitimate competition in what it does so well, it doesn't overcharge its customers (as our local monopoly on the garbage certainly does). In fact, this garbage pick-up is a gratis service.

God's Garbage Disposal Unlimited is available anywhere, anytime to pick up the untold tons of emotional and spiritual garbage generated from the Lord's people. There is no limit to how big a load of garbage, or how small, GGDU will handle. The motto of this industry giant is "have garbage, will pick up." The Chief Executive Officer of GGDU, the Lord God Himself, stands behind the service.

If this description of God as the divine "garbage man" shocks you, join the crowd. But be thankful that it's true, however strange it sounds. After all, if the Lord refused to deal with the garbage from our lives, where would we be? In the emotional and spiritual "sewer"!

Amazingly, the biggest problem GGDU encounters in doing this job is that it can't convince customers to put out their garbage consistently. With a lot of believers, no amount of reminding or pleading will get them to deal with the garbage in their lives. They just keep shoving it back into the deep recesses of their hearts, apparently clueless that this compacted trash can get out of control.

The Apostle Paul clearly understood the need for Christians to get rid of the garbage from their past. After having developed something of a résumé of his life before becoming a believer in Jesus Christ (Philippians 3:2-6), he now discusses how to deal with the garbage from that past (3:7-9). That will lead to further dynamics in his "Process for Recovery," as seen in the following densely packed verses (3:10-16).[1]

In the passage before us (3:7-9), Paul is working from the realization that Christians need to collect and put their garbage "out front" for the Lord to pick up. In order to aid this early part of the process, the apostle advises how to discern what is garbage, which needs to be promptly disposed of, versus what is of lasting value. This is his overarching principle: *The garbage in your life is most clearly seen in the light of your commitment to Christ.*

THE PROFIT-AND-LOSS SHEET

As I mentioned earlier, I made a bad decision to major in accounting in college. The only significant factor I can point to in making that choice is that I enjoyed taking bookkeeping in high school.

Maybe the saddest, or at least most ironic, part of that decision is that I seem to have retained more from the basic high school bookkeeping course than I did from all the college accounting courses I took during the following four years. At least I remember generally how to set up a balance sheet and a profit-and-loss statement.

There is no reason for thinking that Paul ever took a bookkeeping course in his life. Still, in Philippians 3:7-8 he does a remarkable job of setting up a spiritual and emotional profit-and-loss statement for his readers' inspection. If I could have been anywhere near as perceptive an "accountant" as Paul, I might be filing tax returns for a living today (I shudder at the thought!).

On his spiritual spread sheet, Paul is figuring his "gain" and "loss" in Christ. He is analyzing the question "How has my huge investment of my life to Christ altered my overall life portfolio?" His bottom-line findings have great implications for all Christians, but particularly for those of us with recovery issues and needs.

For a solid basis of comparison, the apostle pulls out his last profit-and-loss statement from the period before he became a Christian. We find a summary of that P & L attached to the end of Paul's Jewish résumé. It primarily relates to his presumed mega-assets of "zeal" and "righteousness."

When Paul writes "whatever things were gain to me" (3:7), that is what he recalled on his spiritual P & L. As a Jew, his aggressive "zeal" had been a tremendous asset. That passionate work ethic had propelled Paul down the fast track in Jewish circles. As he puts it in Galatians 1:14: "I was advancing in Judaism beyond many of my contemporaries among my countrymen, being more extremely zealous for my ancestral traditions." Paul was a rising young star, and his stock was skyrocketing accordingly on the Jerusalem religious stock exchange.

But don't overlook Paul's massive "righteousness" asset! In external appearance, Paul was as above board as you could get in regard to keeping the Mosaic Law. This "blameless" behavior made him a Mr. Clean candidate for any responsibility that required a spotless reputation.

Actually, these tremendously impressive individual assets are even more formidable in tandem. When you put religious aggressiveness and spotlessness together, what do you come out with? An overdrive "go-getter" with integrity, a very rare breed throughout history. The pre-Christian Saul had been well on his way to cracking the Jewish religious "Fortune 500."

THE NEW SPIRITUAL MATH

Although I did not turn out to be a good accounting student in college, I had been an excellent student at an earlier stage in foundational math skills. To this day, I am proficient enough at basic math that I figure a lot of things in my head, occasionally beating a calculator to the answer even on longer problems.

Frustratingly, though, this asset in basic math skills has not always been profitable in helping my children with their math homework. It's not that I've forgotten how to do the problems. It's not that I can't explain that procedure to my kids. The problem is the newer ways they teach the students to solve the problems today.

Call me a traditionalist in such matters, if you like, but it seems more than a coincidence to me that "the new math" emerged near the period of heavy drug experimentation in the 1960s. Some of this stuff seems like it was flown in from the dark side of the moon!

But my kids are being tested on their ability to use "the new math," and if I'm going to be able to help them I've got to get with the new program.

Similar insight dawned on Paul sometime after he became a Christian. Upon review of his extremely impressive earlier P & L, containing "whatever things were gain to me" at that point, he completely revises his previous assessment. Even knowing this passage as well as I do, it is still something of a shock for me to hear Paul draw his conclusion: "I have counted as loss" all these things "for the sake of Christ" (Philippians 3:7).

This reassessment is even more profound than the effect on property taxes in California caused by the famous Proposition 13 broadside of the tax revolt. What radical new standard was behind Paul's rethinking of his previous spiritual assets and liabilities?

We can think of this total reorientation as a spiritual parallel to the new math. Even though some of my criticisms of that new approach are legitimate, the fact is that part of my problem is simply that I'm not used to looking at math that way. It's a new ballgame, and I'm naturally resistant to newness and the related change in me that newness requires.

The description in Philippians 3:5-6 strongly implies that Paul was also naturally resistant to change. His head-on collision with the Risen Christ on the Damascus Road began the reorientation process that included "An Introduction to the New Spiritual Math."

It soon became more and more obvious to Paul that he could not continue with the same values he had stood for before he came to know Jesus Christ through faith. That tension would have been akin to what we call in counseling "cognitive dissonance."

The apostle courageously moved his entire outlook in the new direction, in spite of the likely emotional pain involved. The things that had been "gain" were now all viewed as "loss," while an entirely new sense of value was beginning to emerge from the ashes of his former life outside of Christ.

DECLARING SPIRITUAL BANKRUPTCY

When a person loses everything, whether in a catastrophe or a bad investment, there are usually few options available other than declaring bankruptcy. The only good news in making that choice is that the bankruptcy courts will normally let a family keep their house and some other essential items. And there is also the opportunity to make a new beginning, difficult though it may be, if people are able to look past their losses.

By his settled decision to "write off" all the supposed profit of his pre-Christian experience, Paul was, in effect, declaring spiritual and emotional bankruptcy.[2] In fact, he went well beyond our normal bankruptcy proceedings because he decided to count *all* things as loss (3:8). In other words, he decided not to keep *anything* from the time before he was a Christian.

With eyes wide open, Paul was boldly choosing to start all over again from scratch at mid-life. Except for his memories of that former lifestyle, all "diplomatic relations" (i.e., attitudinal and behavioral links) with the past were hereby consciously severed.

This was a right and necessary step for Paul to take. It was, how-ever, anything but easy. We have all seen people undergo conversion and leave their former lives behind—whether drinking, drugs, or cult involvement—only to return to those troubles when the pull of the past is too strong to resist. They simply can't make the break on a gut level.

FACING THE LOSS OF THE PAST

There is nothing overtly emotional in Paul's words in Philippians 3:7-9. But nothing in the passage is bound up in an emotionless straitjacket, either. Had these words been uttered by anyone else, they would doubt-less have carried heavy emotional overtones.

It's worth considering how someone else would feel in a situa-tion such as Paul describes in Philippians 3. The average person would greatly regret losing financial advantage, position, power, and prestige. Yet even that loss of things and influence could be surpassed by other factors that might well be stronger yet.

What if a hard decision you made cut you off completely from beloved family members and longtime friends? Emotionally, it would be virtually impossible not to view your formative choice as a kind of self-imposed exile. That would be incredibly hard to work through and avoid blaming yourself for causing the relational and emotional separation.

If the average Christian would react to the major reorientation por-trayed in Philippians 3:7-8, why wouldn't Paul do so at least to some degree? To claim that Paul felt *none* of those emotions is tantamount to claiming that he felt nothing at all. And *that* certainly doesn't wash!

A SNAPSHOT OF PAUL'S PAINFUL LOSS

There is one scriptural passage that may provide a window into the ongoing situation between Paul and his family long after he made his decision to count all things from his pre-Christian life as loss. In Acts 23:16, "the son of Paul's sister" warns Paul of a Jewish plot to kill him. Though nothing beyond this context is known of Paul's sister or nephew, much less the rest of his family,[3] this is enough to impart significant insight from several angles.

For example, Paul apparently did not call on his sister or nephew to help him while he was in custody in Jerusalem. This may indicate that he did not know they lived there, but it's more likely that he did not expect to receive any help from them no matter what the circumstances.

Paul had proven to be a great embarrassment to the family. After having been raised for the latter part of his growing-up years in Jerusalem and educated there to be a strict Mosaic Law-abiding citizen, Paul had, in the eyes of Jewish onlookers like his family, gone completely off the deep end in becoming a Christian.

It's highly unlikely that Paul's family ever had a change of heart regarding his religious reversal. In his defense before the Sanhedrin recorded just before the plot to kill him, Paul still referred to himself as "a son of Pharisees," a completely nonsensical description if his family no longer followed that tradition.

It might be argued that either Paul's sister or nephew had become Christians somewhere along the way. Although that is possible, it is not at all plausible because of the way that Paul's nephew got word of the plot to kill Paul. His information would not have been gossip on the streets of Jerusalem because of the solemn nature of the "oath" taken by the conspirators, as well as the urgency brought on by their promising not to eat until Paul was dead (23:12-13). The nephew would almost certainly have heard of the plot from someone in this close-knit group or one of "the chief priests and the elders" (23:14), who secretly authorized the plan (23:15). This meant that Paul's nephew was trusted with insider information because it was taken for granted that he would never undermine the plot.

This move to save Paul's life apparently means that at least some in his family still cared whether he lived or died. But they could not condone his beliefs and abandonment of strict Pharisaical Judaism. Even though his family was still there, he had, for all practical purposes, suffered a total "loss" in the extremely painful relational sense, as with everything from his pre-conversion period.

Adding this very realistic relational dimension to Paul's loss not only allows him to be more "human" in our understanding, it makes it much easier to draw applicational parallels from Philippians 3:7-8. For those who must make painfully hard decisions either to become Christians and begin biblical recovery or to put a period of Pharisee-like Christian denial behind them, it cannot be expected that family and friends will always understand the life-changing decisions and their implications.

As with Paul, it is absolutely necessary to give some sense of closure to the former period by chalking it up as a "loss," even if that has to happen over and over again until it finally sticks.[4] Some may experience more grief than others. But all who seriously pursue biblical recovery must come to terms with their own personalized sense of loss as soon as possible.

THE MOST VALUABLE THING IN LIFE

What is the most important or valuable thing in a person's life? The answer, of course, would vary greatly from person to person. But it would also change drastically for each person from one point to another in his or her life, particularly at a time of loss.

To make this point, I will ask you to think with your mind *and heart* of San Antonio, Texas, early on a Sunday morning in September 1986. As a fire blazes from the house on the corner, a gentle rain begins to fall. The dazed owner of the house stands drenched in the middle of the yard, wearing his pajamas and robe, having sent his wife and children to a friend's home nearby.

What were *my* thoughts that fateful morning as I watched our recently renovated house go up in flames? Although the quick response of the San Antonio Fire Department combined with the rain to put out the fire much sooner than expected, I was convinced that we had lost the whole ball of wax. All the furniture and keepsakes that Cathy and I had collected during our years of marriage were in that house.

But what *really* mattered at a time like that? Was it our clothes, the appliances, the older furniture that Cathy had carefully purchased over the years, or even her long-desired hardwood floors?

None of those things entered my mind for more than a fleeting instant. Why? Because I was so thankful to be alive and to have gotten my family out of the fire safely. I was comforted in knowing that our lives were intact and that our insurance would cover much of the loss.

Genuine comfort was also available for the Apostle Paul because he knew that he had gained even more than he had lost. His "comfort" was not a big insurance payoff, though there definitely was a valuation factor involved: "the surpassing value of knowing Christ Jesus my Lord."[5]

In response to the question, "What is the most valuable aspect of your life?" most Christians would immediately pledge allegiance to

Jesus Christ. They might even rapidly add that Christ is "the life" (John 14:6). But, there might be some very different answers if the question was, "What do you *feel deep inside* is the most valuable part of life?"

If people were down-deep honest, many would name some physical possession or human love, or something else they can touch and hold. Before you rip such people for giving such an answer (or me for asking such a question), remember that this inquiry does not ask about personal belief or surface commitment. It simply seeks to get to the heart of the matter.

For people in denial, or even for those who are beginning to face recovery issues in their lives, there is not much of a pipeline connecting the surface world of thought and theology with the subterranean realm of deep emotions. There really is very little conscious awareness of whether your deeper feelings are marching in step with what you profess "up top."

This, I'm convinced, is where a lot of the problems associated with what I am choosing to call a "crisis at mid-life" (CML) have their genesis. After deep emotional inconsistencies fester for a number of years, they blast their way to the surface of the consciously unsuspecting personality. What seems like an emotional blowout in the form of a CML is actually a slow leak that has been there all along at the core.

The reverse of this negative process can be used effectively to help new and recovering believers take hold of the "surpassing value of knowing Christ Jesus my Lord" in the depths of their heart. Instead of a slow leak *out* of the Christian's deepest inward emotions, it is equally possible to develop a gradual leak *into* those innermost recesses of the heart, implanting the surpassing value of knowing Christ at that deep level. That can be done through whatever means are effective in bringing the person's emotions into play, such as music, on the subject of the treasure of knowing Christ.

A STINK NEAR THE LOST-AND-FOUND BOOTH

Never one to mince words, Paul draws a graphic contrast between the "surpassing value of knowing Christ" with what he had lived for before becoming a Christian. In comparison to his relationship with Christ, the glories of his unsaved Jewish lifestyle were "rubbish." There is even the considerable possibility that this term should be translated as either "garbage" or "dung."[6]

Please understand that Paul is not seeking to be crude or overly critical of the Jews. Rather, he is underlining the wonder of Christ, who can fill up many empty (or undeveloped) places in the hearts of hurting believers. In comparison to Him, all the things we once lived for are fit to be trashed.

If you are in the process of realizing that your former spiritual life may well have been a spiritual garbage heap, you don't have to feel lost and alone. There is a lost-and-found booth nearby that is manned by none other than Jesus Himself. He is there both for your sense of "gain" related to Him and your protection.

As a child, every year I went with my family to the Mississippi State Fair. At least once, I remember getting lost from the family. Once I realized what was going on, I headed for the lost-and-found area. On the way there from wherever I had strayed, I distinctly remember smelling some of the foulest odors imaginable from the nearby livestock barns. But it was worth going by those barns to get to the lost-and-found booth and be reunited with my family.

Similarly, Paul was willing to recall the stench from his former lifestyle because of the joy of being "found" in Christ after so many years of being "lost."

The painful problem at this point for believers with serious recovery issues is that they tend to feel down deep that their background "stinks" so strongly that Christ is offended. When He meets them at the lost-and-found, they expect to see revulsion on His face—the "I smell a rat" look.

We could hardly be farther from the truth. When the Lord looks at a Christian, even one with the saddest or most traumatic life experience, He chooses to focus on the "righteousness" that He makes available to the believer in Jesus Christ.

RIGHTEOUSNESS ON LOAN

In the last several years, conservative radio talk-show host Rush Limbaugh has taken the country by storm. You don't have to agree with him in order to be entertained by his offbeat sense of humor. Among his novel recorded publicity statements played during station breaks is "Rush Limbaugh, with talent on loan from God."

Although the tone is cocky, perhaps even arrogant, his point is completely legitimate—even if he is not serious. *Everything* we have is from the Lord, including our abilities. That particularly extends to the incomparable gift of righteousness received through faith in Christ.[7]

If righteousness could be earned, those able to do so would be at least as self-righteous as Rush Limbaugh is cocky. But since it can't be earned, the focus shifts to righteousness that is "exchanged" for faith.[8]

Believers with recovery issues need to stop and listen carefully to these words. If true righteousness cannot be achieved by keeping the Mosaic Law (Philippians 3:9) or other kinds of works (Ephesians 2:9), then we must strive to stop all our dysfunctional attempts to earn acceptance at any point in the justification (becoming a Christian) or sanctification (growing in the Christian life) "recovery process."

Though it is deeply ingrained in us to try to earn acceptance through our works, this outlook has never really worked, even at the human level. It will not get us to first base with the Lord! That is the hard, but gracious, reality Paul is laying out in Philippians 3:9.

THE GRATEFUL HANDS OF FAITH

One of my happiest images to apply to God is the All-State Insurance slogan: "You're in good hands. . . ." Closing my eyes, I can see the large, powerful, but gentle hands from that long-running TV commercial.

This sense of balanced strength and sensitivity was one of the few deep-down positive "pictures" of God that I can recall when I began my recovery process. Most of my other ways of looking at God were colored by my problematic relationship with my dad or were highly abstract. But because Dad had large but unusually sensitive hands, and because he did not abuse me with his physical strength, that image stuck.

In both Philippians 3:9 and the All-State hands analogy of God's strong but gentle dealings with His people, another set of hands also comes into play. They are smaller, human hands, and in effect they accept the offer of protection from the larger ones. They respond to the overwhelming, undeserved grace they receive with empty hands of gratitude and with hand-in-hand trust.

This is a confusing transaction to people with recovery issues who have been forced to pay some sort of emotional, often physical (if not monetary), price almost every step along the way in their lives. But it is possible to learn to accept sincere gifts from the Lord—no strings attached!—and it is possible to learn to trust Him step by step, even relatively late in life.

Think about it this way, as deeply as you can allow these word pictures to sink in: Wouldn't you be insulted if you offered a loving gift to someone and that person tried to pay you for it? It takes away the joy of giving when the receiver insists on paying the price-tag. And in this case, the price is much too high for any person to afford: the death of the sinless Son of God on the cross.

If you have ever longed for a heartfelt gift from someone who really loves you, your heart's desire is fulfilled in God's gift of righteousness in Christ. This is much better than a fleeting dream or a wish! It is *reality,* now and forever, as you extend your empty and grateful hand of trust to the loving Father. You can trust Him to be there for you.

SORT YOUR GARBAGE FOR PICK-UP

Among the relatively few times during childhood and adolescence when I felt at all close to my father was while working with him as a team. A lot of times my clumsiness and lack of natural mechanical ability created a tension with the precise engineer in Dad. Thankfully, though, that was not always the case.

We did work together consistently on the early morning newspaper route my brother and I delivered. That holds some very precious "pattern" memories for me. He also had the two of us help him one summer to dig ditches and lay pipe in the mobile home park he had developed from scratch. Even that back-breaking labor in the steamy Mississippi sun is a special memory, mostly because we were functioning as a team, each doing our part in the necessary process.

As I recall the physical disagreeableness of being a ditch digger and pipe fitter, I realize that it was more than offset by my great emotional and relational gain. As a result, I even become willing to participate more in my heavenly Father's garbage business.

Actually, He doesn't ask you and me to do very much. As we clean out our blocked emotions and continue to "count all things" outside of Christ as not only "loss" but "rubbish," He requests that you and I sort through it for what can be recycled as positive memories.[9] The rest goes on the curb for daily pick-up service (with a heavenly smile!) from GGDU. It is the emotional version of the environmentally sensitive thing to do.

10
DYING TO LIVE AGAIN

Make no mistake! For many people, including a substantial number of Christians, the question of whether to embark on recovery is an unavoidable life-and-death issue.

This is true in two senses: (1) If they continue "life" the way it has been, they will probably experience "death" earlier and differently than they might have otherwise; (2) even if they do pursue solid biblical recovery, it will require "dying," in a very real sense, in order to "live" the truly new life that the Lord makes available.

When it gets right down to it, that's a pretty one-sided choice. If staying in the same malfunctioning *dis*comfort zone strictly because it is a known quantity is going to speed up your trip to the graveyard, why sit there and let it happen to you?

Sure, the other route has the smell of death attached to it also, and even a lot sooner. But it makes all the difference in the world! With the biblical recovery approach, *you can rise from the "ashes" of your former existence through the resurrection power of the Lord Jesus Christ.*[1]

DEATH WISH

We know that some individuals with severe problems (usually related to recovery issues) are either openly suicidal or manifest an apparent death wish. They pursue their life in such a destructive or dangerous manner that death will almost surely come sooner than later.

This situation can be seen as a bizarre "fast forward" angle on the strongest effect of the curse God rendered on the human race because of sin: death. But this version of it is doubly tragic, because even though "it is appointed for men to die once" (Hebrews 9:27), there are far better ways of getting to that point than the breakneck speed that stops only at crash and burn.

Although there are a number of Christians who are immediately suicidal,[2] many more have a sort of "slow-motion death wish." Let's not kid ourselves about this: You can crash your car and die almost as easily driving forty miles per hour as you can careening along at over one hundred. One crash may not be quite as dramatic as the other, but either way you're dead.

The sad reality of this analogy is that we are much more willing to try to do something to prevent future automobile fatalities than to head off emotional crashes on the rocky and winding highway of life. All it takes is a few car wrecks to catalyze action such as reduced speed limits, traffic signs and lights, and beefed-up traffic patrols.

But all too often, when Christians succumb to a "terminator death wish" it triggers simply a collective "Too bad!" That is followed up with such profound preventive measures as telling the next candidate for self-destruction, "You know you're not supposed to feel that way!" and sending him or her packing. This is one of the very few responses that actually makes "Go in peace, be warmed and be filled" (James 2:16) look sensitive and caring.

PAUL'S STRATEGY

There is another part of this life-and-death discussion that must be faced if we are going to traffic in reality. Logic would imply that, given a viable alternative, most people would choose the route of limited short-term discomfort followed by great relief, rather than a death wish (even the slow-mo variety). But logic seems to be on the endangered species list in our society these days.

Although many believers desperately need recovery, a large proportion will remain in teeth-clenching denial (frequently enraged that someone would dare mention the possibility). Almost as sad are others who will honestly own up to their needs but will not lift a finger to work toward constructive change.

How can I be so sure of these responses? Partly because I have merit badges for skills in denial and passive avoidance from earlier stages of my life. Partly because a rapidly growing number of believers, including many pastors and other evangelical leaders, are coming forward out of a very similar experience. Partly because, through doing a lot of outside speaking engagements, I am consistently encountering people who are starting to face painful recovery issues—but the others in their relational system are either wearing flak jackets or struggling like a fish on a hook to keep from landing in the boat.

In Philippians 3:10-11, Paul provides a strategy for the power that can deliver us from death-wishes and denial:

> That I may know Him, and the power of His resurrection and
> the fellowship of His sufferings, being conformed to His death;
> in order that I may attain to the resurrection from the dead.

This power channel is so revolutionary that it goes beyond supercharged. It is fully *supernatural* in its power generation—which guarantees all the spiritual horsepower we need to navigate the up-and-down terrain on the road to recovery.

In order to focus the power flow properly, Paul chose a profoundly simple center-facing structure.[3] It works from the outside layers, both of which deal with the resurrection, to the core elements, the sufferings and death of Christ (3:10-11).[4] Table 10.1 (page 140) depicts this "ABBA" structure.

The design of the power strategy that Paul presents in Philippians 3:10-11 is no accident. Clearly, we are intended to pay very close attention to *how* he lays out his ideas in order to get the full force of *what* those ideas are and what they mean for our minds and hearts (possibly very heavy hearts).

Lead-in clues abound as to the purpose of the inverted structure of Philippians 3:10-11. For example, Paul's net value is totally based in "the surpassing value of knowing Christ Jesus my Lord" (3:8). He is intensely focused on his process to "gain Christ" (3:8) and "be found in Him" (3:9).

In saying "that I may know Him" (3:10), Paul is going deeper applicationally on the same subject. He already knows the Lord quite well, but he longs to get just as close as possible. Nothing short of a real "through and through knowledge" is enough.

Table 10.1
Through Death to New Life:
The "Centered" Recovery Structure of Philippians 3:10-11

According to the Apostle Paul, really "knowing Christ" (3:10a) includes a deep understanding of:
    A—"The power of His resurrection" (3:10b)
    B—"The fellowship [Greek: *koinonia*] of His sufferings" (3:10c)

With such in-depth understanding, you are in the process of:
    B'—"Being conformed to His death" (3:10d)
    A'—In order to "attain to the resurrection from the dead" (3:11)

The bottom line: Deep identification with the sufferings and death of Christ is the "doorway" to resurrection power in this present life and the stabilizing hope of our future resurrection.

This is the way it is in good marriages and strong friendships. You get all the way to the core of the other's being, which may be very unlike your own personality. But the relationship can still grow over time. Knowing someone else, and being known, is at once the most vulnerable and the most honored position two persons can be in with each other.

How is Paul suggesting that we can get to know Christ in the closest possible way in this life? By walking a mile in His moccasins. The inverted structure is pointing to the two places where the Lord Jesus has been that you and I need to visit if we want to have close communion with Him and tap into the recovery power He makes available.[5]

Wait! Before you call your travel agent, let me explain: The two locales are the Cross of Calvary and the empty tomb, where Jesus' dead body had been for three days. You won't need to take the trip to Jerusalem, though, unless you are going for another reason. I've been to both traditional sites, and as great as it was to see each, I'm not at all sure that it propelled me along very much in a growing full-orbed "knowing" (intimate closeness) of my Lord.

Actually, you can go to both the Crucifixion and Resurrection sites inside your heart. Sure beats even discount plane fares! But there is a different kind of price to be paid, and it is not cut-rate. That "price" is a portion of suffering, then spiritually dying and "taking off the graveclothes," not unlike the spiritual side of what Jesus Himself did that first Good Friday and Easter.

Here's the main point of Paul's strategy for dying to live again: *You get to know Christ most closely in this life through suffering, dying to your pre-recovery life, and rising to the occasion of your new life.* I wouldn't necessarily suggest this for a fun-and-games outing. But, I would suggest that it is an "outing" (climbing out of your rut of denial or avoidance) that offers a more healthy, truly enjoyable life of growing in your "knowing" of the Lord (3:10).

REALLY KNOWING GOD

As a younger Christian, I was strongly influenced by J. I. Packer's modern classic *Knowing God*. Of the goldmine of wise insights in that amazing book, some of the most profoundly helpful are found in chapter 3, aptly titled "Knowing and Being Known." These insights can help us plumb the depths of the Apostle Paul's goal to know Christ.

Packer summarizes "knowing God" in three bottom-line points: "personal dealing"; "personal involvement, in mind, will, and feeling"; and "grace."[6] All three of these areas are closely related to recovery issues. But the point about "personal involvement" in regard to *emotions* is critically important if believers are to be healthy and balanced.

Since I have been in recovery myself, as well as pursuing in-depth study of biblical recovery, Packer's thoughts about the necessity of personal emotional involvement with the Lord have echoed over and over in my mind and heart:

> We must not lose sight of the fact that knowing God is an
> emotional relationship, as well as an intellectual and volitional
> one, and could not indeed be a deep relation between persons
> were it not so. . . . Ignorance of it argues that, however true a
> man's thoughts of God may be, he does not yet know the God
> of whom he is thinking.[7]

Packer's assertion implies in the strongest way that the surface knowledge and application approach of many Christians today is not a real knowledge of the Lord, just "passing acquaintance." Although they are true believers, they could be considered *dysfunctional believers* because an entire dimension of their most important relationship is seriously lacking, if not virtually absent, in their lives.

What is the answer to this serious emotional deficit in a believer's relationship with Christ? It is closely related to "the power of His resurrection and the fellowship of His sufferings." Let's look at what this *resurrection power* really is and how it can help us draw closer to the Lord in true intimacy.

RESTART POWER

I hate dead car batteries. But my family has had a lot of them, and so I never have much opportunity to get "rusty" about dealing with car batteries. A couple of frustrating repeated episodes have almost pushed me over the edge into the craziness of Southern California bumper stickers. Mine would read, "Love Me, Love My Jumper Cables."

At least I can take some comfort in the fact that God stays very current in handling spiritual jumper cables. As Paul wrote,

> God, being rich in mercy, because of the great love with which
> He loved us, even when we were dead in our transgressions,
> made us alive together with Christ (by grace you have been
> saved), and raised us up with Him, and seated us with Him in
> the heavenly places, in Christ Jesus. (Ephesians 2:4-6)

Basically, what this wonderful passage is saying initially is that the merciful and gracious love of God prompted Him to jump-start our dead spiritual batteries in Christ. Unfortunately, Paul's point about new life is where many people, myself included for many years, stop reading.

If you don't continue, you miss an important key to how God jump-starts your emotional relationship with Christ: His resurrection power (Philippians 3:10) and its outcome. That's what "raised us up with Him and seated us with Him in the heavenly places" (verse 6) is all about.

Here are the main points for a biblical recovery perspective:

(1) Renewed life in Christ is a life in which Christ has *been there* for the believer from the beginning (2:5). (2) Renewed life in Christ is empowered by coming out of Jesus' empty tomb *together* (2:6). (3) Renewed life in Christ means getting to sit *next to* Him in the throneroom (2:6).

Each of the mental images that Paul chose in this passage is ultra-personal. This description of the wonder of salvation is also a picture of the loyalty and consistency, shared exciting experiences, and sense of "specialness" that most people with deep recovery issues did not receive in their growing-up years. They long for such a relationship but assume it is not possible for them.

If you feel that way, give Christ an opportunity to restart that dead battery cell that did not activate properly when you became a Christian. The exhilaration of running out of that tomb hand-in-hand with Jesus is incredible! And you will never get over that guest-of-honor seat with your name on it in the heavenly throneroom!

SUFFERING AND CONFORMING

The heart of Paul's inverted "death and life" structure in Philippians 3:10-11 is the face-off between "the fellowship of His sufferings" and "being conformed to His death." Both are clearly related to Christ's death on the cross. Both are also strongly related to recovery.

People with dysfunctional or abusive backgrounds find it difficult to feel valued and accepted. The word translated "fellowship" could just as easily be rendered "partnership."[8] We could say that Christ is offering each believer a partnership arrangement with Him.

Admittedly, a partnership in Christ's sufferings sounds less appealing than a partnership in a Fortune 500 company. I have done just enough suffering to know I don't like it. So I have a hard time getting pumped up for Paul's prescription in Philippians 3:10 to suffer and die.

However, Paul and Peter agree that the way of suffering is also the road to glory over the long haul.[9] There is something in it for each recovering believer in the future. But there is also the opportunity to gain a deeper understanding of how Jesus "felt" during all the suffering He endured on the way to and on the cross.

The mirroring phrase "being conformed to His death" (3:10)

almost surely looks ahead to "conformity with the body of His glory" (3:21). If full emotional identification with Christ's sufferings is the recovery road that leads to glory, then a glorious body is a significant part of what is at the end of the road on which Christ and the recovering believer travel together.

Another aspect of "being conformed to His death" is that Jesus Christ actually *died*. If recovering believers get that message loud and clear and order their own emotional-behavioral casket, it will greatly enhance their ability to make a clean break with the old life. Biblical recovery can proceed across the board only if the old life really "died" instead of just passing out for a short period.

COMMENCEMENT RECOGNITION

In our society, the primary focus of academic commencement exercises is to celebrate the course of study just completed. That has always seemed a little odd to me, because the term "commencement" actually means "beginning." But this popular usage has now broadened the term to mean the end of one phase and the beginning of another.

I suspect that Paul might have been comfortable with a similar understanding of "that I may attain to the resurrection from the dead" (3:11). The difference would be that there are two phases of the resurrection of the body framing the believer's renewed life.

Looking back at the power of Christ's resurrection provides the sense of "beginning" a whole new phase of life. Looking ahead to the future resurrection, in which our present limitations and needs (which in 3:21 Paul calls "the body of our humble state") will be transformed, we encounter the sense of joyous completion. Then, and only then, will we finally have our act together in the fullest sense. That is the ultimate goal line at the end of the field of spiritual and emotional battle.

RISING TO THE OCCASION OF NEWNESS

"Newness" is a particularly slippery concept. Sometimes it means brand new, as in a new baby. Other times it means renewing a cycle we have been through before, as in "Happy New Year!" Sometimes it is partly both, as in a new coat of paint on our car or house. Sometimes it is even a fresh start where none was expected, as in "a new lease on life."

Biblically, there is no doubt that a believer is, in a very important sense, "a new creature" (2 Corinthians 5:17). The problem is figuring out how "new" this renewed life in Christ is, because the term is variously used with almost all the shades of meaning listed above.

Paul provides an important insight in Romans 6:4 when he uses the illustration of baptism to portray the reality of "newness" in the believer's life. He strikingly parallels the two in these well-known words: "Therefore we have been buried with Him through baptism into death, in order that as Christ was raised from the dead by the glory of the Father, so we too might walk in newness of life."

There are several points in this verse that help us understand death as the doorway to a new life beyond. First, the resurrection body of Christ, the first element in Paul's comparison, was not *totally* new. The general appearance and scars of Christ's resurrection body provided continuity with His pre-cross body. Similarly, in the radical newness there will be factors of continuity in the person entering biblical recovery.

Second, Paul's use of the word *might* ("so we too might walk in newness of life") indicates that there is a responsibility on the part of the believer to put the newness into force.[10] This "newness of life" will not be forced on us. To enter into it, we must hold up our end of the deal.

Third, the "walk" idea is a step-by-step outworking that, along with the commands of the following verses, adds up to a "process" that is quite close to the way biblical recovery moves forward.[11] Since Paul commonly uses the same term elsewhere for the responsible growth process, this understanding seems highly likely.[12] There seems to be growth expected in the "newness" Paul speaks of in Romans 6:4.

Recovery is a life-and-death issue. But we must enter the new life through the gate of death. Through a deep, wholistic identification with the death of Jesus Christ on the cross, we can experience the power of His resurrection, looking ahead to the final goal beyond the end of the recovery process: that we may know Him, and the power of His resurrection and the fellowship of His sufferings, being conformed to His death; in order that we may attain to the resurrection from the dead . . . the transformation of our humble state into conformity with the body of His glory.[13]

LOOKING BACK,
THEN MOVING ON

I have to admit to being forgetful on occasion. But I don't think I'm in danger of being an absent-minded professor. I remember content for teaching and preaching very readily, as well as people's names, telephone numbers, and a lot of information nobody else seems to remember. That kind of memory makes me a feared Trivial Pursuit ace!

On the other hand, I would walk out of the house to work every morning without something I need if Cathy didn't hand it to me at the door or put it on the seat of my car. I'm almost as bad with short grocery lists. If I don't write down a three-item list, I'll probably forget two of the items—if I even remember to go to the store.

What's going on here? How can a mind that remembers some things so well forget so many things in other areas? Is it really possible to be selectively forgetful?

Aside from brain damage, I have absolutely no idea whether there's a physiological cause that creates such an effect. But there is a plausible way to explain selective forgetfulness as a condition we bring on ourselves. It involves *what* we like to think about, not *how* we think.

In my observation, most people have little difficulty remembering what they're interested in or what is of great importance to them. The memory begins to fail when it's something that distracts them from priority work or activities, or something they just don't care much about.

This is embarrassing for me to admit, because the logical conclusion is that the grocery list must not be very important to me, or I would remember it. And it's even worse to apply that reasoning to owning up to forgetting somebody's birthday almost every year.

I'm just glad I'm not the guy I sat next to at a dinner recently. In his twenty-five years of marriage, this obviously intelligent and capable man had *never* remembered his wedding anniversary. "Selective forgetfulness" won't stretch quite that far!

Things are quite a bit different, however, when you really *want* to forget. It seems as if certain painful mental images and the related emotional upheaval will not leave you alone. Those are times when you would give a lot for an "on call" streak of forgetfulness.

The Apostle Paul understood very well the need to forget and to remember in a healthy, balanced way. He knew that even though it's not good that you forget to remember, *it is absolutely necessary to remember to forget.*

By the time his letter to the Philippians reaches 3:12-14, Paul has covered a lot of ground in developing his pattern for recovery. He has warned his readers not to put confidence in their bare human abilities (3:3-4) by honestly sharing the "mask" he wore as a nonChristian (3:5-6) so that none of his readers would be similarly tempted. He has disclosed the process of he went through of reevaluating everything in his life (3:7-9). He has revealed that all the things he had lived for outside of Christ he now considers garbage, and he treasures everything related to knowing Christ in an intimate way as precious. The Cross and the Resurrection are the points at which the Lord desires to meet His people for close fellowship (3:10-11).

MODESTY OR REALITY?

Because of the straightforwardness and strength of Philippians 3:2-12, it would be easy to conclude that Paul had now finished getting his act together. But the apostle hastens to add a note of reality on the subject of recovery: "I haven't arrived!"

That is exactly what Paul is getting at when he writes, "Not that I have already attained *it* or have already become perfect" (3:12). Some may see this as modesty—perhaps even false modesty—on the apostle's part. But Paul is not shy in declaring his own relative degree of maturity (3:15).[1]

The reason Paul felt he had to make these balancing statements was the presence of the Jewish legalistic false teachers in Philippi. If they weren't claiming to be out-and-out perfect already, they apparently were leaving the impression that they were within hailing distance. Paul did not at all want to be perceived as being overly confident "in the flesh" (3:4) or arrogant in any way. So he told the truth about himself, even if it might somehow make him look less impressive in comparison to the false teachers who were troubling the church.

In our media-saturated culture, we are often tempted to judge our leaders according to slick, carefully contrived public images. When we begin placing all the importance on the packaged effect, we are susceptible to the same kinds of dangerous influences that the false teachers in Philippi had on their hearers. We begin demanding an artificial perfection, which reinforces others' attempts to supply it.

Where is the modeling of the biblical reality that the Lord's delight is in strengthening the weak? Where is the fearful realization that the exalting of "greatness" at the human level is flat-out asking for a major siege of humbling from the Lord?[2]

I wonder what kind of response there would be in the Church today if Paul suddenly stepped out of a DeLorean time machine. I fear that just as soon as he cataloged all his weaknesses and problems—so similar to the kinds of recovery issues many Christians are working through today—he would "fall from grace" in the eyes of the masses who focus their attention on human strength and giftedness instead of divine grace.

REDIRECTED ZEAL

This reference to Paul's refreshing forthrightness about his weakness does not mean he was less productive than those who flexed their "ministry muscles" for all to see. In fact, in repeatedly saying "I press on" (Philippians 3:12,14), Paul provides important clues to productivity for many on the road to recovery.

The word translated "pursue" in 3:12 and 3:14 is the same as the one underlying "persecutor" in Paul's résumé of his unsaved life (3:6).[3] The point seems to be that Paul was no less "zealous" and committed in his new life as a Christian than he was in his old life as a nonChristian Pharisee. His energy level had been redirected and "repackaged" in a healthy and balanced outlook. He no longer was motivated by the apparent perfectionistic tendencies and volcanic rage that had preceded his conversion.[4]

By application, this seems to mean that those who are go-getters before entering recovery can in the process of recovery achieve a balance in which their energy level is fully utilized to the glory of God. This is in keeping with Paul's guideline that believers are expected to be "zealous for good deeds" (Titus 2:14). The concern, of course, must be that such "high-voltage" Christians do not fall back into the old unhealthy patterns. That's where consistent honest self-examination and accountability comes into play.

We should recognize, however, that every believer does not have the same level of God-entrusted "talent" (Matthew 25:15). Comparing ourselves with other believers or copying them runs counter to the way the Body of Christ was designed.[5] It is a hard lesson for those with recovery needs to internalize, but no other Christian can properly occupy the "niche" in the Body that God has prepared for you.

GRASPING AND HUGGING

When Paul spoke of being "laid hold of by Christ Jesus" (Philippians 3:12), he probably had in mind the decidedly firm grasp exerted by Christ on the Damascus Road encounter.[6] Sometimes it takes the "tough love" grip of intervention—the human counterpart of what happened to Paul—in order to stop someone's self-destructive lifestyle and direction and point him or her down the path to recovery.

Paul's experience is a classic biblical pointer to the need for such intervention when a person's behavior is on the edge, especially if that person is in any sort of leadership role. The credibility of some ministries has ended up being completely lost because obviously out-of-bounds behavior has been overlooked. Also, the individual who is acting out this extreme behavior can frequently be stopped before the snowball rolling downhill hits bottom.

It seems to me that the "laying hold" imagery in Philippians 3:12-13 can also apply in terms of a "hug." Surely if we can create contemporary versions of the "holy kiss" (Romans 16:16) in a culturally appropriate "holy hug" or "holy handshake," then a "hug" is not misapplying the idea of a firm, loving grasp in Philippians 3:12-13. If anything, it may capture the flavor of the concept even better than the stark "laying hold."

Feel the powerful emotional force of the "hug" here. Having been held tightly and lovingly in the grasp of the Lord Jesus (3:12), Paul "presses on" (3:12,14) to return that infinite and eternal "hug" (3:12), but he's not there yet (3:13).

This is such a special word picture for me! To the best of my recollection, my dad did not hug me much when I was a child. Largely as a result of that early deprivation of physical affection, I grew to adulthood feeling uneasy about open affection. If it hadn't been for my wife's affectionate nature and efforts to break through my reserve, I might have stayed that way indefinitely.

Years ago, long before either Cathy or I knew about recovery, we decided that we would always respond this way to our kids: "Kiss 'em and hug 'em until they shove you away, then kiss 'em and hug 'em some more." Sure, I know that when they get to be teenagers, they will probably be embarrassed by some of the mushy stuff. But I hope that most of the battle over where they go for appropriate affection will be won by that delicate point in their lives.

So far, so good. Our kids respond well to our parental affection and are more naturally and spontaneously affectionate than I had thought possible. I am very thankful both for Cathy's hugs, which started the ball rolling in a healthier direction in my life, and for the Lord's "hugs," which make the "sufferings" (3:10) on the road to recovery much more bearable.

Don't ever underestimate your ability to make a real difference in others lives simply by giving them a safe, caring hug. If they're really hurting, you could make their day!

TWO FOR THE PRICE OF ONE

One of the most confusing parts of this section in Philippians is Paul's wording "one thing" (3:13). In the very same verse he seems to turn around and list *two* things instead of just one: (1) "forgetting what lies behind," and (2) "reaching forward to what lies ahead."

The explanation is really quite simple, though. Perhaps you recall the mint commercial that started off with the apparent disagreement between "It's a candy mint!" and "It's a breath mint!" The seeming conflict was resolved with "No, it's two, two, two mints in one!" You didn't have to choose between a candy mint and a breath mint. You got both for the price of one.

That's basically the way it is in Philippians 3:13. "Forgetting" and "reaching forward" are two sides of the coin of the "one thing" Paul had chosen to do in pressing on in Christ. There is absolutely no contradiction or conflict between them. As we will see, taking these *two* steps actually enables Paul to be even more "single-minded."

Paul could not have pursued "reaching forward" as he needed to if he had not already been involved in "forgetting what lies behind." It is also true that "forgetting" biblically is incomplete if the "reaching forward" does not accompany it or closely follow it.

These two phrases are biblical Siamese twins, joined at the heart. Though capable of separate consideration, they are not intended to be fully separated. It is not healthy for either aspect if the other one is not there and active.

FORGETTING: AN OVERLOOKED EVANGELICAL HERESY

In this enlightened era, the term *heresy* is hardly ever tossed around except in church history classes. This tolerant attitude brands almost anyone who would call a viewpoint "heretical" as a hard-liner, a legalist, or a divisive voice.

But I will gladly accept that calculated risk of possible derision. The heresy that I want to take to task is the popular "forgive and forget" teaching in many evangelical circles today.

The argument goes something like this: "You haven't really forgiven until you have fully forgotten" (this refers to both the person and the incident involved). To back that assertion, appeal is made to Philippians 3:13 and the supposed way God does things. Then there are some "long jumps" through the Bible to justify the presumption that God "forgives and forgets."

These long jumps are worthy of an Olympic gold medal. One common stretch cites the declaration in Jeremiah 31:34 that the Lord will "remember" His people's sins no more, along with other passages indicating that God will somehow take their sin far away. From that inadequate biblical base, the quantum leap is made to the mind-boggling conclusion that the Lord literally erases the tapes in His divine memory banks that were storing records of now forgiven sins. The applicational force is that Christians are expected to "go and do likewise."

DOES GOD "FORGET"?

This "forgive and forget" teaching is a classic Swiss-cheese position: it's full of holes.

For example, it assumes (though the assumption is rarely stated) that the only viable definition of "forgetting" is selective amnesia. Yet this definition clearly crumbles when applied to God's Person. If He "forgets" even one little piece of data for even a millisecond, He is not fully omniscient (all-knowing). We're left with the implication that God is "semi-omniscient"—clearly a non-orthodox (heretical) position!

This kind of "god" would be flying as blind as you and I in many areas because there is so much sin He has to forgive! In the case of forgiving Judah's sin that caused the Babylonian Exile (Daniel 9:1-20), God would have to blank out huge chunks of history that had been totally dominated by sinfulness.

Second only to the rotten tomato that this strange concept throws at God's character is the emotional devastation that it promotes wherever people take it seriously.

In coming to grips with my own recovery, I have become aware of how sad and unhealthy it is for anyone to engage in repression, or "stuffing away their feelings"—which for me had blocked out all except a handful of my childhood memories until less than two years ago.

But this is exactly the kind of insidious "application" that modern-day false teachers of the forgive-and-forget heresy are foisting on unsuspecting Christians. In essence, they are telling us that we must blank out all memories of whatever we need to forgive in order for it to be a done deal. The corollary is that if the memory comes back up in our mind and emotions, we didn't really forgive as we should. In most cases, the assertion is that we should retain no memory whatsoever of the person(s) or event when we "truly" forgive.

Think about the effects of this attempted voluntary amnesia on its unsuspecting victims. Suppose we do succeed in pulling off this mental blackout to some degree. What is the outcome? We have been set up for the next time. If we don't remember what happened in the past, we certainly couldn't have learned anything that will help us face similar circumstances in the future. We'll get blind-sided over and over again.

But there is also the mountainous problem of repressed memories and emotions. Since we know that full memory loss happens only with severe amnesia and brain damage, we can be sure that those memories will surface again at some unpredictable point in the future. But after being under lock and key for so long, they will be bound and determined to make us listen to them. They will pull out all the stops to make us acknowledge their pain and confusion. It will be as if a massive tornado developed in our soul that is now intent on leveling everything in its path.

In other words, we simply cannot "forget" the way these teachers tell us we must. So one of several things will happen, and none of them are any good. We might admit our difficulty only to be told that we are spiritually "out of it." Or we will simply keep it a secret that we lack the ability to erase our mental and emotional blackboard. We will go on, deeply troubled, wondering what is so terribly wrong with us that we can't forget on demand. Or, worst of all (but not uncommon), we will become so frustrated and disillusioned about not being able to "forgive and forget" as we were taught to do that we will give up on the idea completely, perhaps blowing off Christianity in the process.

Which of these is the tragic outcome? All of the above. That's like asking, "Which is the tragic disaster, the San Francisco earthquake or the L.A. riots?"

Which of these calamities is easy to repair? None of the above. They put the emotions of open, committed believers through the ringer by pressuring them to call into question every attempt at forgiveness in their lives.

Let me say this in the most direct way. If you care one iota about biblical legitimacy or the spiritual and emotional well-being of yourself or other believers in Jesus Christ, you will stay as far away from the "blank out the tapes" view of "forgetting" as you can get! To do otherwise is to flirt knowingly with out-and-out theological heresy and to open yourself to tremendous, unnecessary emotional upheaval.

REMEMBERING TO FORGET

It's high time to nail down the true biblical approach to "forgetting what lies behind" (Philippians 3:13). We will do that in two ways. First, we will look carefully at Paul's meaning based on the context. Second, we will develop the balanced biblical position by contrasting it with an orthodox, but short-sighted, evangelical alternative. (See table 11.1 for a visual display of these two approaches.)

Table 11.1
How to "Forget" Painful Memories: Two Competing Approaches

NATURAL FLATLANDS APPROACH	HUMAN PERSONALITY IN GOD'S IMAGE	SUPERNATURAL DEPTH APPROACH
"Erase" (repress) logical thoughts privately (alone)	*Mind:* What did it look like?	Sort out and learn from your transparent thoughts (Psalm 139:1-4)
Ignore the "heart of the matter"	*Emotions:* What did it feel like?	"Defuse" and disconnect the explosive feelings from the thoughts (Ephesians 4:31-32)
Determine it will be a "one-shot deal"	*Will:* What can I do about it?	Choose to "stick with it" until the process is complete (present tenses in Philippians 3:12-14)
Bottom line: instant, surface "coverage" (just below the surface)		Bottom line: eventual release and deprioritizing (to "inactive status")

In Philippians 3, Paul initially shows that he has not forgotten anything meaningful from "what *lies* behind" (3:13) by reciting the résumé of his unsaved life. However, he does appear to have learned a great deal from sorting out these memories.

In 3:7-9 Paul talks at length about the process of reevaluating his life. All the things that were once on the assets side of the ledger got moved over to the liabilities side. All the items that rode at the top of the priorities list plummeted to the bottom. He has totally *deprioritized* all that lay behind in his life.

Finally, in 3:10-11 Paul has put all the old stuff to death. When he died spiritually with Christ on the cross, he knew he couldn't take it with him. So he left those memories and other things that lay behind at the foot of the Cross for the Lord's garbage pick-up crew to handle. In a very real sense, they would *die off* without his emotions to feed on.

What does all this add up to? Paul's concept of "forgetting what lies behind" (3:13) is basically *remembering* with a few additional wrinkles. When you remember those past people and events, you must: (1) carefully learn from what happened (3:2-6); (2) consciously deprioritize those things to the point that they simply no longer have a "vice grip" on your head and heart (3:7-9); and (3) consistently "casket" those memories at the foot of the Cross (3:10-11). I'm not saying that they won't die a lingering death. But if you don't feed them with the upheaval of your emotions, which give them destructive life, they will fade into being just memories as you release the hurtful emotions attached.

This view is in contrast to a (supposed) orthodox evangelical alternative I referred to earlier. I call it the "flatlands" approach because it is a simplistic treatment of surface emotions. Basically, it teaches that you simply "will" to forgive, and it's done. Then you can "forget," as easily as if you were making a cup of instant coffee. Presto!

Besides ignoring the depth of human personality made in God's image, the flatlands approach obviously creates many emotional problems—almost as many as the forgive-and-forget angle. But even though it's not a heretical position, it's biblically imbalanced. What really tips the scales in revealing its flaws is the parade of present tenses throughout Philippians 3. Clearly Paul is referring to a process.[7] These step-by-step present tenses are describing a *recovery process*.

FULL SPEED AHEAD!

Where does this recovery process leave us? Released from the emotional albatrosses from around our necks. Liberated from the concrete shoes that have immobilized us in the past. Free to stretch forward toward that finish line where the Lord is waiting with the prize for all who have stayed the course. Free to chart that upward course to all He wants us to be in this life and then on to literally heavenly points beyond. That is the end of the road for biblical recovery: the Lord's victory stand!

LIVING IT UP . . . OR DOWN?

To the average person, the expression "living it up" is roughly equivalent to "sowing your wild oats." It means more than just having a good time, and it often implies borderline or over-the-line behavior that can have embarrassing or even tragic consequences. This irresponsible conduct, which is a far cry from the exhilarating sense of "living it up," frequently forces the oat-sower to "live it down" over the long haul.

An important message here is especially appropriate as we wrap up this study of biblical recovery for Christians. Believers with painful background issues who are growing through recovery will experience continuing temptations to take some "wild oats" detours, or even to chuck the whole thing, when life is particularly confusing or depressing. At times like this, the key thing to remember is: *If you don't live responsibly during your recovery process, you will probably live to regret it.*

Does this mean that fun has no part in the process? Does the word *sober* have to mean being somber and deadly serious? Is laughter always in danger of crossing out of biblical bounds?

LIVING IT UP, BIBLICALLY

As King David began his journey of biblical recovery after his devastating affair with Bathsheba, he passionately asked the Lord to restore to him the joy of his salvation.[1] In another of his prayerful hymns that was probably written around the same difficult time, David advises his fellow worshipers, "Be glad in the LORD and rejoice, you righteous ones, and shout for joy, all you who are upright in heart" (Psalm 32:11).

David's words do not sound somber to me. Neither do such sentiments of the Apostle Paul as "rejoice always," "rejoice with those who rejoice," and in the wider context developed in the second half of this book, "rejoice in the Lord."[2]

So, although the biblical recovery process clearly requires consistent responsible living, we should not mistake it for a joyless existence. As was implied in the last chapter in our exploration of what Paul meant by pressing on toward the goal for the "upward call" of God (Philippians 3:14), it is entirely possible to live it up, or to live your life on the upswing in Christ, without going to a destructive extreme.

Life without laughter is a sad substitute for really living. I don't think it's stretching the text in Philippians 3 to assert that an appropriate balance of fun and responsible living fits very well with Paul's concept of a mature "attitude" (3:15) and living up to the level "which we have attained" (3:16).

NOBODY'S PERFECT, BUT . . .

Christians realize that the truism "nobody's perfect" is an imperfect claim. Jesus Christ, the unique sinless God-Man, was indeed perfect. Other than Christ, however, the list is as short as it can possibly be: no names.

Since "nobody (else) is perfect," what does that say about the rest of us? Well, it certainly says that we are imperfect. But it does not specify the degree of imperfection—or, if we turn the tables, the degree of "completeness" or "maturity" short of perfection.[3]

Even though Paul has already approached this subject (although from a different angle) in Philippians 3:12, it's important to pay attention to what he does with it in 3:15. At first glance it seems that he has changed his mind or even contradicted himself in a space of only three verses. In 3:12 he is at pains to make it clear that he is not perfect ("Not that I have already obtained *it,* or have already become perfect"), but in 3:15 he places himself in a category that sounds arrogant or elitist ("Let us . . . as many as are perfect").

Has Paul joined the ranks of the egotistical? Is he now claiming to add a few names other than Jesus, including his own, to that short list of those who are perfect? Will the real Apostle Paul please stand up?

Never fear! Paul has not rejoined the ranks of the perfectionists from which he was converted. Nor has his spiritual and emotional evaluation of his stock gone through the roof. He is simply comparing himself to two different standards by using the same fluid concept.

In Paul's letters, the word translated "perfect" (3:15), *teleios,* sometimes has the precise flavor of "grown up" (1 Corinthians 14:20). This related meaning allows me to illustrate what the apostle is doing through a side-by-side comparison from my own recovery profile.

Physically, I was an early bloomer. I reached my adult height and frame at the age of fifteen (although my weight has fluctuated). So from one angle, I was much more "grown up" at an early stage than many of my classmates.

Emotionally, I was a very late bloomer. Whatever I looked or sounded like on the outside was not an accurate indication of the deep-down reality of my largely frozen personality on the inside. I was a scared little child thrown out into the deep water of an adult world with no real idea how to swim. From that perspective, I was a far cry from being grown up.

As my example shows, the exact shade of meaning attached to a flexible idea depends primarily on the vantage point. In Paul's case, he had initially compared himself to what he would be at the end of the "race" of this life (3:12). Looking at things from that absolute, final angle, he most certainly had not "arrived." In 3:15 he is presenting himself as a sort of walking, talking recovery model for those behind him on the race course.[4] From that relative, comparative angle, Paul was a good deal closer to "arriving" than many of his friends in Philippi or his readers today.

When these different but complementary uses are understood, they can be very helpful for those in recovery. It is realistic to admit that nobody "arrives" in this life. On the other hand, it is encouraging to know that we do graduate to higher growth planes over time and that others behind us in the recovery process can find in us a helpful, even stimulating, model for the recovery road ahead.

ATTITUDE ADJUSTMENT

The slang usage of "attitude" today usually means a bad attitude or an attitude problem. If you say to someone, "You have an attitude," it almost always means that person needs to change his or her outlook immediately, if not sooner.

This same meaning was attached to the popular phrase of a few years ago "attitude adjustment." Back in those days, which were also my stoic days, I treated the idea of an attitude adjustment in a flippant way. Adjust my attitude? No problem. It's about as complex as setting the thermostat for the amount of heating or cooling you want. What's the big deal?

But now I realize that attitude adjustment *is* a big deal. That's because when you change a person's attitudes, you significantly change the person. The effects of the change may be good or bad, but that person is no longer the same person he or she was before. Whoever said "Clothes make the man" obviously didn't know much about the shaping power of attitudes.

Paul, however, does understand the crucial importance of a proper attitude (3:15).[5] He knows full well that a person's recovery, or even a relatively healthy person's deeper growth in Christ, is dead in the water without major "attitude adjustments" from earlier outlooks. In fact, the wording "have this attitude" (that is, the attitude developed as Paul's "Process for Recovery" in 3:7-14) reflects the apostle's settled conviction that even relative "maturity" in Christ requires going this route of attitude adjustment, rocky and painstaking though it may be.

The implication in Paul's point here is vast, as much for Christianity-at-large as for its recovering segment. By the markers of "therefore" and "this attitude" (3:15), Paul is, in effect, asserting that to be a proper model of spiritual maturity, a person must embody a "recovery lifestyle." Also, with the phrase "as many as" (3:15), Paul is limiting (or expanding) the number in the group to those who have made the necessary attitude adjustments.

This understanding of spiritual maturity cuts right through the widespread emphasis on appearance in so many evangelical circles today. It would be a much easier task to encourage the shattered lives of unbelievers and believers alike along the path to recovery if we had more leaders who set healthy—that is, truly biblical—models of spiritual maturity. But too often, a lot of "diseased" attitudes and behavior (such as legalism, perfectionism, refusal to face "garbage," and "playing God"[6]) pass for what it means to have your act together spiritually.

Don't think for one second that I'm throwing rocks at a glass house I haven't lived in! To my shame, over my years as a pastor, I have unconsciously left those false impressions of maturity. I was long guilty of clinging to the appearances and activities of a "maturity" that had little internal reality because there was tragically little depth and internal understanding.

It has taken some major-league, and pretty painful, attitude adjustments for me to move in the direction of the kind of biblically mature attitude Paul is commending to the Philippians. I certainly haven't "arrived" by a long shot—but even five years ago I would have been hopping mad in my denial of the words I just wrote.

RIGHTING THE WRONG ATTITUDES

From a legal and political standpoint, every person in a free society has a "right" to his or her own opinions and related attitudes. From a purely pragmatic angle, some of these legally protected personalized outlooks are foolish and shortsighted. But everyone has an equal right to hold them.

For the believer who is committed to the truth of Scripture, there are no "equal rights" for attitudes. Some are right and some are wrong.

In his letter to the Philippians, Paul seems to be anticipating wrong attitudes in his readers as he encourages them to have the right attitude. He is diplomatic but direct: "if in anything you have a different attitude" (3:15) implies that he is challenging all the *wrong* attitudes about the process of maturity as expounded in 3:12-14.[7] Because Paul was committed to speaking the truth in love (Ephesians 4:15), he did not shrink from a "tough love" approach in confronting his readers.[8]

But it is significant that, having been blunt about wrong attitudes (Philippians 3:15) toward the biblical recovery process (3:2-14), Paul does not push things any further at this point. He leaves the ball back in his readers' court: "if in anything you have a different attitude, God will reveal that also to you" (3:15).

Paul apparently does not pursue this point because he is realistic enough to recognize the tenacious nature of denial. You can call a spade, a spade until you are blue in the face, but a person entrenched in denial will continue to call it a pickax or a garden hoe if it helps stave off the onslaught of the discomfort zone. Only the Lord can dissolve that kind of stubbornness.

I know this because I was a much-decorated veteran of the wars of denial before I resigned my commission two years ago. I was a master of this sad combination of spiritual resistance, pride, and fear of change.

It took divine intervention to move me toward righting my wrong attitudes. In fact, I'm now convinced that my experience of the recovery process was right in line with the expectation of divine intervention that Paul lays out in Philippians 3:15.

Among other events, my traumatic experiences with resigning from a pastorate in San Antonio and our house fire were evidence of God turning up the heat. But it took the loss of my father, the loving prompting of my wife, and a miserable bout with viral pneumonia to open a crack in my shield of denial. Only then did I begin to recognize and admit my painful recovery issues.

When I finally began to see the light in all this, it was a monumental revelation in my life! As I have searched the Scriptures, I have meticulously clarified and undergirded that personal insight from biblical revelation.

These two aspects of personal revelation and biblical revelation are part of how God reveals wrong attitudes to us. Based upon Paul's usage elsewhere in his letters, it's clear that he has these aspects in mind in 3:15 as he assures his readers of God's revelation. For example, in Romans 1:16-18 Paul refers to the eye-opening nature of the gospel message of justification by faith in Christ alone as well as the intensifying "wrath of God" against resistant (i.e., denying), unbelieving humankind.[9] Paul indicates that both aspects are "revealed," meaning "from God." Also, in Ephesians 3 Paul refers to the biblical content that the Lord imparted to him to write down as Scripture, as "revelation" that "has now been revealed" (3:3,5).

Why shouldn't a caring God who wants His people to be healthy, balanced, and increasingly mature "turn up the heat" in our denial cocoons until we are flushed out into the full light of recovery? As Paul indicates, we can expect that He will use His supernatural laser of *timeless* Scripture and *timely* personal revelation.

DON'T DROP BACK AND PUNT

As a child in the late fifties and early sixties, I stayed glued to radio broadcasts of the classic football match-ups between the University of Mississippi and Louisiana State University. That annual game often decided the Southeastern Conference championship, and a couple of times it ended up delivering the national championship.

Although both squads were very good offensive teams, they were known for their tremendous defense. I understood that point, but to this day I disagree with the choices the coaches sometimes made to punt on second down. It still seems completely backward to me for a team that is supposed to be driving forward to the goal to purposely give up the football so the other team can take it the opposite way. Those decisions seemed to me, if not irresponsible, at least highly counterproductive.

When believers facing recovery issues choose to "punt on second down" on their life commitments and responsibilities, they yield ground to the Devil and his team, who are in an invisible do-or-die struggle with the Lord's people.[10] If we fumble the ball or, more accurately, just turn it over, Satan will score points against us, our family, and the Church.

When Paul writes, "Let us keep living by that 'standard' to which we have attained" (Philippians 3:16), he is essentially advising his readers to hang on to the ball. We can almost hear the apostle as player-coach hollering, "Hang in there! Let's move it toward the goal!"

In spite of all the painful difficulties and dangers for the Christian that John Bunyan so vividly portrayed in his classic work, he still chose to name it *Pilgrim's Progress*. I freely admit that times of confusion and even depression are reality for those in recovery. But an open-ended lapse in responsibility and testimony is out of bounds. The guidelines for biblical recovery strike such a balance of grace and truth that they disallow timeouts for blaming others for our failure to move forward.

THE GROWTH UNDER YOUR BELT

About ten years ago I was approached by a junior high youngster who wanted to show off a new vocabulary word. He earnestly asked me his rhetorical question, "Pastor Luter, you have a pretty *sedimentary* job, don't you?" I, of course, knew that he meant *sedentary*. I chuckled under my breath and, with a glance at the "silt" beginning to gather at my waistline, answered with a straight face, "You could say that."

At the end of Philippians 3:16 Paul speaks of the level of Christian growth "to which we have attained." Even believers with major recovery problems have managed to attain a level of spiritual growth well beyond where they were as brand-new Christians. So as they open themselves up to deal with their painful internal or relational issues, they have this stabilizing basis of growth to fall back on.

This maturity level can provide a platform on which to build future growth—even if later you sadly discover, as I did, that a few planks in your launching pad were rotting with more garbage than growth. So be encouraged: that spiritual growth under your belt is a welcome development.

A REVIEW RIDE OVER THE RECOVERY LANDSCAPE

As we conclude our journey across the territory of recovery, let's review where we've been by taking a "helicopter ride" over our primary passages, Daniel 9 and Philippians 3.

I hope that our view of the parts and the whole in both these amazing sections of God's unerring written Word will never look the same again because of the in-depth interpretive and applicational trip we have made together.

Dare to Be Like Daniel

Far from the lofty stereotype of a godly statesman and prophet unaffected by all that swirled around him, Daniel exhibited a clear pattern of recovery. I have called what Daniel went (and grew) through "trauma at life's bookends" (table 2.1, page 28) because the struggles he faced in his formative years shared similar issues with the struggles he endured late in his life. According to what Scripture presents, the entire middle section of Daniel's life was remarkably placid.

The best clues that we possess as to what was going on inside this remarkable man of God emerge from what comes out in what I have called his "Prayer for Recovery" (Daniel 9:4-19) and its immediate context. Table 12.1 summarizes the most important ways we can apply the insights from Daniel's incredible prayer for our own process of recovery.

Table 12.1
Principles for Prayerful Recovery:
Learning from Daniel's "Sackcloth and Ashes"

DANIEL 9:1-20
1. Be open to a more in-depth understanding and application of Scripture that can fuel your prayers for recovery (9:2).
2. Be willing to express a heartfelt sense of grief for past sins that affect you, even if you are not directly responsible (9:3).
3. Make honest confession and repentance the cornerstone of your prayers focused on recovery (9:4,20).
4. Appeal directly to the righteous, compassionate, forgiving, and infinitely loyal character of the Lord God (9:4,7,9,15-16,18-19).
5. Face your paralyzing sense of shame related to sinful, destructive past events transparently before the Lord (9:7-8).
6. Purpose firmly and consistently to obey the Lord's scriptural "boundaries" as "good faith" from your side of the relationship (9:10,13).
7. Ask God to act in answer to your prayer because of who He is and who you are in relation to Him (9:15-19).

Follow Paul's Prescription for "Forgetful" Living

Although Paul's dysfunctional background is clear-cut (Philippians 3:2-7), the process by which he dealt with that "baggage" has not been as clear to students of Scripture up to this point. Neither have been the general contours of the "crisis at mid-life" (CML) through which he became intimately acquainted with the sufficiency of God's grace and power in times of weakness.

All theories of instant, or point-in-time, healing of Paul's emotional and background issues go up in smoke after careful study of the "Process of Recovery" that the apostle lays out in Philippians 3:2-16. The major applicational "trigger-words" are in the present tense, almost certainly indicating an ongoing process of coming to grips with what lies behind as well as ahead (3:13).

Table 12.2 (page 166) summarizes Paul's principles that we can apply to our process of recovery.

How's the Renovation Going?

I can chuckle at the TV show *Home Improvement* because I have played that game before. We had substantially renovated our house in San Antonio just a short time before it went up in flames. Like Tim on *Home Improve-*

ment, we had tried to do things in the most reasonable way financially and time-wise. For the most part, we were reasonably successful.

Table 12.2
Processing Biblical Recovery:
Learning from Paul's Crisis at Mid-Life

PHILIPPIANS 3:2-16
1. Honestly evaluate yourself to see whether you are "putting up a front" or relying on your own strength or ability instead of the Lord (3:2-4).
2. Admit openly that external "zeal" and religious conformity can never take the place of internal reality in Spirit and truth (3:3-6).
3. Rework your life "profit-and-loss statement" through the lens of faith in Christ, even if it means declaring spiritual "bankruptcy" in regard to the past (3:7-9).
4. Sort out the "garbage" from your past, sifting out what is of lasting value and leaving the rest for garbage pick-up (3:8).
5. In your pain, identify closely with both the sufferings and the resurrection power of the Lord Jesus Christ (3:10-11).
6. Release your painful emotions by remembering "what lies behind" and then cutting loose and moving full speed ahead as Christ calls you (3:12-14).
7. Be a model for less mature and hurting believers by responsibly standing firm in your growth during your own recovery (3:15-16).

But we made one big mistake in our renovation work, and it cost us dearly. We took an acquaintance's advice in hiring a particular contractor to bring the electrical wiring in this older house up to the municipal code specifications. This guy was indeed cheap, but we realized that we had paid outrageously for his cheap wire when it turned out to be the cause of the blaze.

I'm not a rocket scientist, but I was bright enough to learn a major principle from that painful debacle: *You can't get away with half-done quickies for very long at the point where the power is supposed to flow.*

This principle applies directly to many of you who are reading this book. You're probably in either one of two quite different places in your life right now.

First, in response to what you have been reading, you may be concluding for the first time (or more seriously than before) that you—like Daniel, Paul, and many other biblical luminaries—have recovery issues to deal with. If so, don't make the mistake of doing it halfway. You could end up "burning" yourself in the process.

Second, you might already have embarked on the voyage of recovery. You may have gotten the wrong impression that I am promoting a "short-cut" to recovery through my emphasis on getting to the heart of the matter and getting through it. I am advocating no such thing. But it is my view that, just as summer-school classes cover the same amount of material in fewer class days because each session is much more concentrated, biblical recovery counseling can develop a more compact and responsive framework for the healing process. That way, the recovery work can still be done in necessary depth while the power of the Holy Spirit is brought to bear, in an unhindered way, on disabled lives, marriages, and families as soon as possible.

Perhaps you feel that your life is like an old house, ready to fall apart. If so, give the Lord a shot at your renovation job. Among many satisfied customers, Daniel, Paul, and I would be happy to serve as very positive references.

A

MARKS OF SAFE-HAVEN AND NOT-SO-SAFE CHURCHES

If you're looking for a recovery-sensitive church in our country today, it is the best of times and it is the worst of times.

It is, joyfully, the best of times because more and more biblically committed congregations have awakened to the legitimate recovery needs (and opportunities) in their midst and all around them. It is, sadly, the worst of times in many areas where evangelical churches are either unaware of (though this is increasingly rare), insensitive to, or hostile to a recovery perspective.

Almost always, the more intense negative responses are partly based on the shortsighted perception that recovery doesn't have a biblical leg to stand on (see chapter 1). Also, numerous churches have witnessed the procedures and effects of extreme secular or even New Age approaches to recovery. In such cases, a degree of biblically informed caution is obviously warranted.

However, the unvarnished reality is that a disturbing number of evangelical congregations, instead of providing healing contexts for individuals who need recovery, are themselves candidates for corporate recovery. Just as it took a period of time for the understanding to take hold that family relationships can be as powerful a "carrier" for dysfunctional behavior as the individual, observers are now beginning to recognize and bring the dysfunctional church family "out of the (evangelical) closet."[1]

While not claiming to be either an expert or exhaustive, I approach this subject from a somewhat unique biblical, pastoral, and personal recovery background. From that perspective, I sincerely believe the following introductory checklist is a valid and helpful way to determine whether a church body needs to seek "group recovery."

Table A.1
How to Be a Dysfunctional Church . . . Without Really Trying

REGARDING PAST PROBLEMS
- *Unsolved problems:* By covering up, denying, or avoiding unresolved past conflicts in the church.
- *Unaccepted responsibility:* By characteristically blaming families or factions that left the church as the cause of problems, even when they are later repeated.

REGARDING PULPIT POWER
- *Manipulative messages:* By preaching or teaching that resorts to a guilt trip or shaming in a consistent manner, even if it is very subtle.
- *Compartmentalized messages:* By preaching and teaching that rarely projects beyond the surface "head knowledge" level, virtually denying or avoiding the emotional and "gut level" dimensions of the image of God in humankind.

REGARDING "PATERNAL" DISTANCE
- *Imbalanced "nurturing":* By either dominating and dictatorial leadership or passive and virtually invisible leadership at the board and/or pastoral level(s).

REGARDING PERSONAL(ITY) SHALLOWNESS
- *"Surface" counseling:* By, as a matter of principle, not encouraging counseling beyond the "take two verses and call me next week" variety, even in cases of fairly clear abuse, trauma, or depression.
- *Plastic "happy faces":* By the strong unstated expectation that you must always answer the "How are you doing?" inquiry with a smiling "Great!" or "Fine!"—no matter how badly you are hurting.

For the sake of clarification and contrast, I will present my description of a healthy congregation last. A healthy church is the virtual opposite of the appearance-oriented "new car showroom" approach sketched in the list above. In terms of basic characteristics, it is a courageous and balanced group of believers committed to running a spiritual "paint and body shop" to repair the relational and spiritual dents or crashes the Lord sends their way.

Table A.2
How to Be a Safe-Haven Body . . . Without Going Too Far

REGARDING PROBLEM-SOLVING
- By facing past and present problems head-on, with a united front.
- By accepting legitimate responsibility for the problem(s) at hand, without taking the fall as martyrs or "automatic apologizers."

REGARDING PULPIT PHILOSOPHY AND STYLE
- By avoiding guilt trips, manipulation, and shaming in preaching and teaching.
- By seeking to minister to hearers' emotions and wills as well as their minds (wholistic biblical exposition).

REGARDING HEALTHY "FATHER-FIGURES"
- By appointing only emotionally honest individuals with growing personalities as positive leadership models.

REGARDING AUTHENTIC SHARING
- By making available in-depth counseling either in-house or through referral to knowledgeable and biblically compatible counselors.
- By making honest, heartfelt answers to painful personal inquiries the rule rather than the exception.

Obviously, there is a high price to be paid for becoming a recovery-sensitive church body. Consequently, it is much easier to avoid the question or deny the skyrocketing number of people (including Christians) with incapacitating recovery-related needs. Happily, there are also priceless dividends that are the spiritual and emotional pay-off from being a safe-haven church. Chief among these benefits are:

1. *Prevention:* heading dysfunction off at the pass through understanding (biblically and behaviorally, in tandem).
2. *Diagnosis:* surfacing existing needs in believers (and unbelievers).
3. *Healing:* intervention, where necessary, and consistently encouraging and motivating the recovery process.
4. *Support:* providing a context of balanced safety and accountability.

B

PREACHING AND TEACHING BIBLICAL RECOVERY: A BASIC CHECKLIST

NECESSARY PREREQUISITES

1. You must clearly understand relevant biblical and counseling principles yourself.
2. You must honestly evaluate your own life and family (both your own household and your family of origin).
3. You should definitely gain agreement (consensus) at the ministry leadership level before proceeding.
4. You should seriously count the cost up front of the pain on the road to greater gain.
5. You should investigate thoroughly where you can "plug in" those who respond for needed counsel and support.

COMMUNICATION/APPLICATION PRINCIPLES

1. Adapt *timeless* scriptural principles for *timely* application to recovery issues.
2. Plan to speak "wholistically" (to the whole person, from the whole Bible).
3. Do not communicate a shaming or manipulative message.
4. Do share a hope*ful*—beyond hopelessness—message.

5. Carefully balance expositional focus on the "hurting" and the "healthy" as seen in the Bible.
6. Carefully avoid either "gutter-izing" or glamorizing biblical characters or situations.
7. Aim prayerfully for the goal of longer-term recovery, realizing that longstanding behavioral patterns are usually "tough nuts to crack."

STYLES OF PRESENTATION

1. *Topical/thematic messages:* If it is legitimate to focus on the biblical topic of "life" as it relates to the contemporary abortion controversy, it is certainly valid to deal with key recovery issues like "forgiveness," "God as the perfect Father,"[1] "denial," or "grace."

2. *Biographical/character studies:* Since part of this book is basically biographical exposition (see especially chapters 2 and 7), it can be used as a model for focusing on biblical characters from a recovery perspective. Fertile ground elsewhere would be Old Testament characters such as Moses, Ruth and Naomi, Samson, and David (and his family). In the New Testament, the Samaritan woman (John 4) and Timothy offer equally intriguing, but very different, studies in recovery issues.

3. *Exposition of a biblical portion or book:* The bulk of this volume is comprised of detailed exposition of Daniel 9 and Philippians 3. A similar shorter recovery series could easily be developed from a section of Genesis, Exodus, Judges, or Ecclesiastes; or Matthew, Galatians, or Hebrews. There is no reason, however, why any of these biblical books, or others, could not be worked through completely from a recovery standpoint,[2] especially if holiday and special occasion messages are interspersed in a longer series.

SELECTED BIBLIOGRAPHY

The following recent works (all but one entry have been published in the last ten years) have been chosen because of their relevance, or broader helpfulness, for the average reader in regard to the biblical or recovery issues addressed in this book, not because of agreement with the author on any point(s).

BIBLICAL APPLICATION

BEERS, Ronald, general editor. *Life Application Bible*. Wheaton, IL: Tyndale, 1988.

   This one-of-a-kind resource provides general applicational insights on every significant passage in the Bible, as well as several other features designed to enhance practical life transformation. Highly recommended!

KUHATCHEK, Jack. *Taking the Guesswork Out of Applying the Bible*. Downers Grove, IL: InterVarsity, 1990.

   This brief book is a goldmine of distilled wisdom concerning the knotty problems of moving from interpretation of the ancient biblical text to application in the modern world.

LUTER, Boyd. "How to Interpret and Apply the Bible." *The New American Standard Study Bible*. George Giacumakis, general editor. La Habra, CA: Lockman Foundation, forthcoming.

This essay provides a compact guide to a basic framework and skills for understanding Scripture at both the content and personal levels.

BIBLICAL COMMENTARIES
AND STUDY NOTES ON DANIEL

ARCHER, Gleason L., Jr. "Daniel." *The Expositor's Bible Commentary*, volume 6. Frank Gaebelein, general editor. Grand Rapids, MI: Zondervan, 1986.

This is the best middle-level evangelical treatment of the book of Daniel currently available. There is, however, relatively little in regard to application.

FERGUSON, Sinclair B. *Daniel. The Communicator's Commentary* series. Dallas, TX: Word Books, 1988.

Beyond his sometimes scanty textual and theological comments, Ferguson provides numerous helpful suggestions of an applicational nature.

LUTER, Boyd. "Daniel." *The Life Recovery Bible.* Steve Arterburn and David Stoop, general editors. Wheaton, IL: Tyndale, 1992.

These notes sparked what grew into the first half of this book and offer a complementary angle for understanding recovery issues in Daniel.

BIBLICAL COMMENTARIES AND STUDY NOTES
ON 2 CORINTHIANS

BRUCE, F. F. *1 and 2 Corinthians* in *The New Century Bible Series.* Grand Rapids, MI: Eerdmans, 1971.

This is a reliable resource volume on these difficult, but crucial, letters in a compact and affordable form.

LOWERY, David. "1, 2 Corinthians." *The Bible Knowledge Commentary: New Testament.* John Walvoord and Roy Zuck, general editors. Wheaton, IL: Victor Books, 1983.

This is one of the most helpful segments in the entire two-volume *Bible Knowledge Commentary* set.

LUTER, Boyd. "2 Corinthians." *The Life Recovery Bible*. Steve Arterburn and David Stoop, general editors. Wheaton, IL: Tyndale, 1992.

    For those interested in tracing recovery themes beyond the discussion of 2 Corinthians 11–12 in this book (see chapter 7), refer to this segment.

BIBLICAL COMMENTARIES AND STUDY NOTES ON PHILIPPIANS

CRADDOCK, Fred. *Philippians* in the Interpretation series. Atlanta, GA: John Knox, 1985.

    Writing from a broader theological context, Craddock presents a warm-hearted and intuitive perspective on Paul's interaction with the church at Philippi.

DAVIS, Barry. "Philippians." *The Life Recovery Bible*. Steve Arterburn and David Stoop, general editors. Wheaton, IL: Tyndale, 1992.

    Helpful compact insights on both the biblical text and recovery issues.

LUTER, Boyd. "Philippians." *The Evangelical Commentary on the Bible*. Walter Elwell, editor. Grand Rapids, MI: Baker, 1989.

    This essay develops the background, structure, and general application of Philippians at a readable level.

BIBLICAL RECOVERY ISSUES

ARTERBURN, Stephen, and David Stoop, general editors. *The Life Recovery Bible*. Wheaton, IL: Tyndale, 1992.

    It's very difficult to continue "denying" that recovery is a biblically based framework after seeing this overarching (Genesis through Revelation) scriptural analysis and application by a team of biblical studies specialists and leading Christian counselors. An essential resource!

HEMFELT, Robert, Frank Minirth, and Paul Meier. *Love is a Choice: Recovery for Codependent Relationships*. Nashville, TN: Thomas Nelson, 1989.

This book provides a wonderful basic introduction to recovery issues, particularly as they relate to a dysfunctional home setting. The principal parties in the nationwide Minirth-Meier Christian counseling organization have proven quite skilled in effectively integrating Scripture and psychology. "Must reading" for beginners.

LEMAN, Kevin, and Randy Carlson. *Unlocking the Secrets of Your Childhood Memories.* Nashville, TN: Thomas Nelson, 1989.

As usual, Leman's ideas are common sense, well-communicated, and intensely practical. (Also available in an inexpensive Pocket Books edition.)

STOOP, David, and James Masteller. *Forgiving Your Parents, Forgiving Yourself.* Ann Arbor, MI: Servant Publications, 1991.

Among the most common, and troubling, of recovery issues is forgiveness. Here it is handled expertly by two counselors, both of whom have a theological degree and ministerial experience.

TOWNSEND, John. *Hiding from Love: How to Change the Withdrawal Patterns that Isolate and Imprison You.* Colorado Springs, CO: NavPress, 1991.

This is the best work available on two-layered intimacy—with other people and with God—from a writer with strong counseling and theological credentials.

VAN CLEAVE, Stephen, Walter Byrd, and Cathy Revell. *Counseling for Substance Abuse and Addiction.* Volume 12 in the Resources for Christian Counseling series; Gary Collins, general editor. Dallas, TX: Word Books, 1988.

The concepts developed in this book and the biblical integration have a much broader application than just alcohol and substance abuse issues. This book should be within reach of every pastor who desires to be sensitive to recovery needs in the years ahead.

NOTES

Chapter 1—Who Needs Recovery?

1. This project was the *Life Recovery Bible,* Steve Arterburn and David Stoop, eds. (Wheaton, IL: Tyndale, 1992). My initial contact with the editorial team was Dr. David Stoop of the Minirth-Meier Clinic West.

Chapter 2—Better Late Than Never

1. My studied opinion is that Daniel himself wrote the book bearing his name. For an excellent, concise treatment of the question of authorship, see Gleason L. Archer, Jr., "Daniel," *The Expositor's Bible Commentary,* vol. 7, Frank E. Gaebelein, ed. (Grand Rapids, MI: Zondervan, 1985), pages 4-6.
2. See Archer, page 6.
3. For the events surrounding Josiah's kingship, see 2 Kings 22–23.
4. For helpful discussion of evangelical perspectives on the vision in Daniel 2, see: Archer, pages 42-49; Sinclair B. Ferguson, *Daniel,* in *The Communicator's Commentary* (Dallas, TX: Word Books, 1988), pages 60-66.
5. The events in Daniel 1–3 probably occurred during 605–600 BC, although chapter 3 could be slightly later. However, the next step forward in the book's chronological sequence (after chapter 4) is Daniel 7, which can reasonably be dated between 556–553 BC

(Archer, page 84).

6. According to Archer, the fall of Babylon (see Daniel 5:30-31) took place in 539 BC, and Daniel 9:1 is set in the following year. It strains plausibility to push Daniel 6 back much further timewise.

7. See Hebrews 12:6-11.

Chapter 3—Biblical Study and Deep Recovery

1. Considering that Daniel 5:31 (in the English text) is placed as 6:1 in the Aramaic text (i.e., leading into the following events), it seems highly unlikely that the lion's den (Daniel 6) and Daniel's "Prayer for Recovery" (Daniel 9), as I have titled it, could have occurred more than a few months apart.

2. The "mourning" period before the final vision of the book of Daniel is stated to be three weeks long (10:2). The emotional upheaval could have been more dramatic just because the time factor is extended, although that is uncertain.

3. Some scholars hold that "Darius the Mede" (Daniel 5:31, 6:28) and "Cyrus the Persian" (6:28) are two names for the same person. The limited biblical support for that position from Daniel boils down to both being called "king" (9:1, 10:1) and the vague "and" construction in 6:28, which could possibly be construed to mean that the reference to Cyrus is intended to explain who Darius is.

   The more likely position is that "Darius" is an honored title for Gubaru, the trusted viceroy of Emperor Cyrus in Babylon during its earlier occupation period—a view well-supported from history. See also the thorough discussion by Gleason L. Archer, Jr., "Daniel," *The Expositor's Bible Commentary,* vol. 7, Frank E. Gaebelein, ed. (Grand Rapids, MI: Zondervan, 1985), pages 16-19, 76-77.

4. See 2 Chronicles 36:22-23 and Ezra 1:1-3.

5. Jeremiah 25:11-12, 29:10.

6. This reality is most clearly apparent in the book of Esther, although it is evident from Ezra and Nehemiah also.

7. Archer (pages 108-109) accurately notes the background considerations from Leviticus and Deuteronomy but does not develop the important interplay to any degree.

8. In my estimation, the most balanced and readable (though it includes scholarly endnotes for those who desire to go deeper) resource on prayer is W. Bingham Hunter, *The God Who Hears* (Downers Grove, IL: InterVarsity, 1986).

9. See chapters 7–12 of this book and my segment, "Philippians," *Evangelical Commentary on the Bible,* Walter A. Elwell, ed. (Grand Rapids, MI: Baker, 1989), pages 1024-1038.

Chapter 4—Getting Beyond a Shameful Situation

1. In the wider recovery movement, one work by John Bradshaw, *Healing the Shame that Binds You* (Deerfield Beach, FL: Health Communications, 1988), is considered something of a classic on the subject. A former Catholic priest, Bradshaw should be read with great theological caution.

    By contrast, most evangelicals will find the introductory discussion in Robert Hemfelt, Frank Minirth, and Paul Meier, *Love Is a Choice: Recovery for Codependent Relationships* (Nashville, TN: Thomas Nelson, 1989), pages 77-92, both understandable and adequate in placing "shame" in its proper recovery context.

2. Besides the prayerful tone of Psalms and much of the wisdom literature, Daniel 9:4-19 is among the longest prayers in the Bible. Significantly, most other longer Old Testament prayers also focus on confession and resolution with the Lord (e.g., Ezra 9; Nehemiah 1, 9).

3. This kind of front and back "bookends" effect is technically called an *inclusio*. It is carefully designed to emphasize a certain theme, or themes, that are developed between the outer structural markers—here the mention of confession in Daniel 9:4,20. Apparently this structure is intended to communicate primarily that one great theme of Daniel's prayer is the necessity of deep, heartfelt confession.

4. See the detailed discussion of this balance in chapter 3.

5. For those interested in the formal question of the authorship of the Johannine epistles, see the excellent new resource by D. A. Carson, Douglas J. Moo, and Leon Morris, *An Introduction to the New Testament* (Grand Rapids, MI: Zondervan, 1992), pages 446-450.

6. The concept of codependency states simply that "no man is an island" in regard to the impact of inappropriate behavior. If a domino falls because of sin in one person's life, it will knock over a domino in the life (or lives) next to that person. For a full-scale but very readable discussion, see Hemfelt, Minirth, and Meier, *Love Is a Choice*.

7. The Significant Other Person (SOP) concept is a key part of explaining codependent relationships. There is never truly healthy emotional interplay in a codependent relational setting.

8. See 2 Kings 21.

9. It is never clearly stated that Daniel was of royal blood. However, it is doubtful that Daniel would have mentioned the royal family in addition to the wider nobility (1:3) unless there was some further significance or implication.

10. Jerusalem was under attack, then decimated in 587–586 BC. Daniel's "Prayer for Recovery" occurred in 539 or 538 BC, slightly under fifty years later.

11. See chapter 6 for a compact discussion of the rebuilding of Jerusalem.

12. For a related discussion, see my entry on how repentance is used in the New Testament: A. Boyd Luter, Jr., "Repentance (N.T.)," *Anchor Bible Dictionary,* vol. 5, David Noel Freedman, ed. (San Francisco, CA: Doubleday, 1992, 1993), pages 672-674.

Chapter 5—Back to the Future, Biblically

1. A helpful overview of the interactive and blending elements of Daniel's prayer is offered by Willem A. VanGemeren in "Daniel," *Evangelical Commentary on the Bible,* Walter A. Elwell, ed. (Grand Rapids, MI: Baker, 1989), page 598.

2. See John Goldingay, *Daniel,* in *Word Biblical Commentary* (Waco, TX: Word Books, 1989), page 225.

3. See chapter 3 for an explanation of what can be known of Daniel's interpretation and application of the twin "seventy-year exile" prophecies from Jeremiah.

4. For a useful, recent summary of how 1 Kings 6:1 provides a historical starting point for dating the Exodus period, see James K. Hoffmeier, "Exodus," *Evangelical Commentary on the Bible,* page 39.

5. See chapter 3 for explanation of the crucial role that Leviticus 26 played as a springboard for Daniel's "Prayer for Recovery."
6. A probable interpretation of the references to Daniel in Ezekiel 14:14,20 and 28:3 suggests praise that puts Daniel in a Hall-of-Fame status. For a summary of a less probable interpretation of these passages, see Victor P. Hamilton, "Ezekiel," *Evangelical Commentary on the Bible,* page 571.
7. The credibility of the entire evangelical sector in the United States was damaged, for example, by the actions of a few high-profile individuals in the Bakker/PTL debacle—which continues to generate national "reproach."
8. The need for responsible living in the midst of a "mid-life" crisis is addressed at length in chapter 7.
9. Goldingay, page 225.
10. There is no record of anyone else in the Babylonian Exile taking the responsibility to ask for God's forgiveness prior to Daniel 9.
11. See Philippians 3:14. Chapter 11 gives a brief explanation of the "call" of Christ in general Christian growth and recovery.

Chapter 6—Another Chance . . . Thank God!

1. See Acts 13:13, 15:37-40.
2. See Matthew 28:19. For a compact discussion of the key passages and various aspects of Christ's climactic command, see my article, "Great Commission," *The Anchor Bible Dictionary,* vol. 2, David Noel Freedman, ed. (New York: Doubleday, 1992), pages 1090-1091.
3. See Acts 4:32-37, 11:22-24.
4. See Acts 9:1-7,26-31.
5. See Acts 9:20-21, 11:25-26.
6. See Acts 15:37-39, Colossians 4:10, and 2 Timothy 4:11.
7. A slightly different but very even-handed discussion of the disagreement between Barnabas and Paul can be found in William H. Baker, "Acts," *Evangelical Commentary on the Bible,* Walter A. Elwell, ed. (Grand Rapids, MI: Baker, 1989), page 908.
8. See J. Knox Chamblin, "Matthew," *Evangelical Commentary on the Bible,* pages 744-745.
9. Chamblin, page 745.

10. See my notes on Samson's life: "Judges," *The Life Recovery Bible,* Steve Arterburn and David Stoop, eds. (Wheaton, IL: Tyndale, 1992).

11. This is the marginal reading in the *New American Standard Bible,* but it is preferable. See also the fresh translation by John Goldingay, *Daniel,* in *Word Biblical Commentary* (Waco, TX: Word Books, 1989), page 225.

12. See the helpful discussion by Gleason L. Archer, Jr., "Daniel," *The Expositor's Bible Commentary,* vol. 7, Frank E. Gaebelein, ed. (Grand Rapids, MI: Zondervan, 1985), pages 124-125.

13. Although such resources may exist, I am not personally familiar with any rigorous, biblically solid, evangelical treatment of the relationship between spiritual warfare and recovery. Particularly with the occult angle in the emerging New Age approaches to recovery, this could rapidly become a critical area in which solid biblical answers must be provided.

14. In the events recorded in Daniel 9, Daniel would have been in his early eighties. See the reckoning of time periods in Daniel's life in chapter 2.

15. Although I think that self-esteem is a valid concept within biblical conceptual boundaries, it should be remembered that the only way to keep self-esteem from becoming almost totally subjective is to link it with God-esteem: both His estimate of you and your estimate of Him.

16. For helpful discussions of this monumental prophecy from two different evangelical perspectives, see Archer, pages 111-121; and Willem A. VanGemeren, "Daniel," *Evangelical Commentary on the Bible,* pages 598-599.

17. I have no reservations about dealing with the content of the prophecy in 9:25-27. I have taught the required course on the exposition of Daniel at least once per school year at Talbot School of Theology for the past five years. But my purposes in this book differ from those in a standard commentary or formal exposition. As fascinating as the prophetic details are, in this context they would likely divert attention from the in-depth applicational focus on recovery issues that I want to maintain.

18. This "bookends" structure, also seen in the recovery prayer (Daniel 9:4,20), is another example of an "inclusio," in which

everything included between the bookends is somehow related to that overarching subject.

19. My candidate for the unifying theme of the book of Daniel is "The Sovereignty of God and the Humbling of Man." Each scene in the book is somehow related to that two-pronged theme.

20. See chapter 11, especially the sections related to understanding "forgetting what lies behind" (Philippians 3:13), the climactic emphasis of this book.

21. Even without the compelling parallel between the unkept Sabbath years of the past, it is virtually certain that the "weeks" (or sevens) refers to years. See Archer's note, page 119.

22. Sinclair B. Ferguson, *Daniel*, in *The Communicator's Commentary* (Dallas, TX: Word Books, 1988), pages 201-202.

23. Archer, pages 112-113. In this broad grouping, some assert that as few as one (usually "to make atonement for iniquity"), and others assert that as many as five, have been fulfilled.

Chapter 7—Surviving a Crisis at Mid-Life

1. The other extended autobiographical passage in the Pauline literature is Galatians 1:10–2:14, which focuses on a very different subject.

2. See 2 Corinthians 11:13,18 and Philippians 3:2,4.

3. Paul would certainly have been over age thirty, a key turning point in Jewish society, when he was given the authority to persecute the church as far as Damascus (Acts 9:1-2). His conversion on the Damascus Road most likely occurred in the mid-thirties of the first century AD. Along with many other conservative New Testament scholars, F. F. Bruce dates 2 Corinthians in AD 56. See Bruce, *1 and 2 Corinthians*, in *New Century Bible* (Grand Rapids, MI: Eerdmans, 1971).

4. See 2 Corinthians 11:32-33. This passage may be speaking of the same incident as that in Acts 9:23-25, though the differences between the two make that uncertain.

5. See James 1:2-3.

6. The verbal form of the Greek word *merimna,* translated as "intense concern" in 2 Corinthians 11:28, has the clear sense of anxiety or worry in key passages like Matthew 6:31,34 and

Philippians 4:6.

My analogy here for the purpose of applicational parallels certainly should not be pressed too far. Earlier in this section of 2 Corinthians, Paul clearly states that the church is engaged ("betrothed") to Christ (11:2). So, if anything, at the human level Paul might be described as the "father of the bride."

For a detailed discussion of the Greek word *zelos,* correctly rendered "jealousy" in 2 Corinthians 11:2, see my article "Jealousy/Zeal," *Dictionary of Paul and His Letters,* Gerald F. Hawthorne and Ralph P. Martin, eds. (Downers Grove, IL: Inter-Varsity, 1993).

7. See 2 Corinthians 11:23-29.
8. See 2 Corinthians 11:30; 12:6,9-11.
9. I will shy away from any speculation regarding the relation of Paul's heavenly revelations to a specific event. Within the known general chronological framework of the great apostle's life, it almost certainly occurred during his years of ministry in Tarsus (Acts 9:30, 11:25-26). Of that period, almost nothing beyond the "tidbit" in Galatians 1:21-23 is known.

    Regarding the timing of these events in Paul's life, there is absolutely no "shoehorning" of dates going on here. It can only be either a coincidence or a factor of purposeful divine providence that Paul hit this major crisis point in his life at the same general age where so many today sail into extremely rough emotional, relational, and spiritual waters.
10. See 2 Corinthians 12:8 and Daniel 9:20-23.
11. See Philippians 4:6-7 and 1 Thessalonians 5:16-18.
12. In my opinion, Paul did not pray just three times, as an initial reading of 2 Corinthians 12:8 suggests. This wording seems to be an idiom for praying repeatedly, much as we would say "over and over and over again" in modern American culture.
13. For a comprehensive discussion of Paul's usage, see my article "Grace," *Dictionary of Paul and His Letters.*

Chapter 8—Getting Beyond the Good Front
1. See especially the procedure developed in chapter 11.
2. The tripled "beware" in 3:2 forcefully warns the reader to avoid this kind of behavior like the plague.

3. The events in Acts 21 took place about AD 57–58, and Paul most likely penned Philippians by AD 62. For the options and evidence for dating Philippians, see my segment "Philippians," *Evangelical Commentary on the Bible,* Walter A. Elwell, ed. (Grand Rapids, MI: Baker, 1989), pages 1035-1036.

4. According to William H. Baker, "Acts," *Evangelical Commentary on the Bible,* page 909.

5. My personal view is that Galatians was written about AD 49, as I have argued in "Galatians," *Holman Bible Handbook,* David S. Dockery, ed. (Nashville, TN: Broadman, 1992). For a plausible later alternative, see Scott E. McClelland, "Galatians," *Evangelical Commentary on the Bible,* pages 1000-1001.

6. Simply put, "legalism" is reliance on external standards (law) instead of true internal transformation as a basis for assessing progress. To a detached observer, obedience may appear legalistic. But the legalist proceeds from the outside in, while a healthy Christian will move from the core of the personality out.

7. The *New American Standard Bible* reads, "for we are the true circumcision." But the word *true* is not in the Greek text. Actually, the force of Paul's point is stronger without it.

8. The Greek word *pneuma* may be referring to the Holy *Spirit* or the human *spirit,* or perhaps even to the spiritual realm in which both are operative.

9. The Greek word *dokeo,* translated "has a mind to," means "seems" (to).

10. See my segment "Philippians," *Evangelical Commentary on the Bible,* page 1044.

11. See Gerald F. Hawthorne, *Philippians,* in *Word Biblical Commentary* (Waco, TX: Word Books, 1983), page 133.

12. See chapter 9 for an explanation of how Paul handled his losses in a healthy way.

13. See Acts 5:34-39, 22:3.

Chapter 9—Garbage In, Garbage Out

1. See chapters 10–12 for my presentation of this ongoing process in a believer's life.

2. "I counted as loss"—the perfect tense of *hegeomai* indicates a past decision with ongoing results, in this case Paul's permanent

declaration of loss in regard to his past life.

3. See William H. Baker, "Acts," *Evangelical Commentary on the Bible,* Walter A. Elwell, ed. (Grand Rapids, MI: Baker, 1989), page 917.

4. Gerald F. Hawthorne comments helpfully on the significant shift from the perfect tense in 3:7 to the present tense in 3:8. See his *Philippians,* in *Word Biblical Commentary* (Waco, TX: Word Books, 1983), pages 136-137.

5. See Homer A. Kent, Jr., "Philippians," *The Expositor's Bible Commentary,* vol. 11, Frank E. Gaebelein, ed. (Grand Rapids, MI: Zondervan, 1978), pages 140-41.

6. According to Kent, page 145; and Hawthorne, page 139.

7. Philippians 3:9; see Kent, page 141.

8. See Romans 3:10,23 and Philippians 3:9.

9. The present tense of "count" in 3:8 nails down this understanding of a continuing process.

Chapter 10—Dying to Live Again

1. Note the parallel between rising from the ashes into a new life (the imagery associated with the phoenix bird of Egyptian mythology) and the "sackcloth and ashes" that represented Daniel's grief over the former way of life of the people of Judah and its sizable impact on his life (Daniel 9:3).

2. This number is far higher than most believers realize. Some would argue that this ideally should not be the case, since a Christian is a new creation in Christ (2 Corinthians 5:17). They might even assert that such people cannot be true Christians. Although the latter certainly may be true for some (Matthew 13:36-43), the biblical reality that is so often overlooked is that the heavy applicational section in Ephesians 4–6 was written originally to a church that could have been expected to be very knowledgeable and mature (Acts 19:8-10). Realistically assuming very little in terms of applicational depth or maturity level, that portion contains directives related to some very knotty emotional and relational issues (e.g., Ephesians 4:31-32).

3. The formal name for an inverted structure is "chiasm." At its simplest, as here, it is a mirroring ABBA effect.

4. A formal display chart of this structure is found in Gerald F.

Hawthorne, *Philippians,* in *Word Biblical Commentary* (Waco, TX: Word Books, 1983), page 145.

5. The word translated "fellowship" in verse 10 is *koinonia* in the Greek, which can also mean "communion" or "partnership".

6. J. I. Packer, *Knowing God* (Downers Grove, IL: InterVarsity, 1973), pages 34-36.

7. Packer, pages 35-36.

8. The Greek word *koinonia* ("fellowship") has the same force here as in Philippians 1:5. There the partnership is horizontal (between Christians). In 3:10 it is vertical (between the believer and the Lord).

9. See Romans 8:17 and 1 Peter 4:13.

10. The form (aorist subjunctive) of the Greek verb *peripateo* ("to walk, conduct your life") may reflect either a coloring of uncertainty or deliberation. See the compact discussion by D. A. Carson, *Exegetical Fallacies* (Grand Rapids, MI: Baker, 1984), pages 75-77.

11. See Royce Gordon Gruenler, "Romans," *Evangelical Commentary on the Bible,* Walter A. Elwell, ed. (Grand Rapids, MI: Baker, 1989), pages 936-937.

12. See Ephesians 4:1,17; 5:2,15.

13. See Philippians 3:10-11,21.

Chapter 11—Looking Back, Then Moving On

1. The Greek word for "perfect" in 3:12,15 is *teleios,* which can be translated "perfect," (relatively) "mature," "complete," "grown up."

2. See Daniel 4:30-37 and 2 Corinthians 12:7-10.

3. The Greek word *dioko* is a present participle in Philippians 3:6 and a present-tense verb in 3:12,14.

4. See Acts 9:1-6. In chapter 7, I identified what seems reasonably clear about Paul's pre-Christian dysfunctional life and personality.

5. See 1 Corinthians 12:4-27. For a formal discussion of this concept, see my article "Christ, Body of," *Anchor Bible Dictionary,* vol. 1, David Noel Freedman, ed. (New York: Doubleday, 1992), pages 921-23.

6. This is pointed out by Gerald F. Hawthorne, *Philippians,* in

Word Biblical Commentary (Waco, TX: Word Books, 1983), page 152.

7. Fred Craddock, *Philippians*, in *Interpretation Commentary Series* (Atlanta, GA: John Knox, 1985), page 63.

Chapter 12—Living It Up . . . Or Down?

1. See Psalm 51:12. For an evaluation of this episode from a biblical recovery perspective, see the notes on 2 Samuel 11 and the personality profile on "David, Michal, and Bathsheba" in the *Life Recovery Bible,* Steve Arterburn and David Stoop, eds. (Wheaton, IL: Tyndale, 1992).

2. See Romans 12:15; Philippians 3:1, 4:4; 1 Thessalonians 5:16.

3. In Paul's wider usage of the Greek word *teleios,* translated "perfect" in Philippians 3:15, the nuance of "mature" or "complete" is the most common shade of meaning. See the longer discussion of this important idea in chapter 11.

4. For a helpful, compact formal discussion of these two uses of *teleios,* see Homer A. Kent, Jr., "Philippians," *The Expositor's Bible Commentary,* vol. 11, Frank E. Gaebelein, ed. (Grand Rapids, MI: Zondervan, 1978), pages 143, 146.

5. It is no coincidence that earlier Paul had challenged his readers to "Have this *attitude* in yourselves which was also in Christ Jesus" (Philippians 2:5, emphasis added).

6. Paul delivers the death-blow to such behavioral heresies in Philippians 3:2-12, as chapters 8–11 discussed.

7. Gerald F. Hawthorne, *Philippians*, in *Word Biblical Commentary* (Waco, TX: Word Books, 1983), page 156.

8. Though the "tough love" concept is a crucial part of a general recovery framework, its balance of firmness and accountability in the context of wanting the best for the dysfunctional "beloved" is completely biblical. In addition, it is patterned after the way God treats His beloved children (Hebrews 12:5-11).

9. For a concise treatment of Pauline usage of "gospel," see my article "Gospel," *Dictionary of Paul and His Letters,* Gerald F. Hawthorne and Ralph P. Martin, eds. (Downers Grove, IL: InterVarsity, 1993).

10. See Ephesians 6:10-13.

Appendix A—Marks of Safe-Haven and Not-So-Safe Churches

1. For example, see David Brubaker, "Secret Sins in the Church's Closet," *Christianity Today,* 10 February 1992, pages 30-32.

Appendix B—Preaching and Teaching Biblical Recovery: A Basic Checklist

1. For fresh and wise insights on this subject, see Phil Davis, *The Father I Never Knew* (Colorado Springs, CO: NavPress, 1991).
2. See the *Life Recovery Bible,* Steve Arterburn and David Stoop, eds. (Wheaton, IL: Tyndale, 1992), for helpful "hints" in applying various scriptural passages to recovery issues.

AUTHOR

Dr. Boyd Luter is chair and associate professor of Bible exposition at Talbot School of Theology and adjunct professor of New Testament at Golden Gate Baptist Theological Seminary. He has fourteen years of pastoral experience. He received his B.S. from Mississippi State University and his Th.M. and Th.D. from Dallas Seminary.

Dr. Boyd Luter was the associate editor for the biblical portion of the *Life Recovery Bible* (Tyndale, 1992). He has contributed to biblical studies and devotional works, including the *Evangelical Commentary of the Bible* (Baker, 1989), the *Anchor Bible Dictionary* (Doubleday, 1992), the *Holman Bible Handbook* (Broadman, 1992), and *Heart Watch* (Victor, 1993). He has also written articles for such periodicals as *Decision* and *Bibliotheca Sacra*.

Boyd and his wife, Cathy, have three children—Joanna, Natalie, and Tim.